ULTRA
PERFORMANCE

PAUL MOORE

ULTRA
PERFORMANCE

THE PSYCHOLOGY OF ENDURANCE SPORTS

BLOOMSBURY

LONDON · NEW DELHI · NEW YORK · SYDNEY

Note

While every effort has been made to ensure that the content of this book is as technically accurate and as sound as possible, neither the author nor the publishers can accept responsibility for any injury or loss sustained as a result of the use of this material.

Published by Bloomsbury Publishing Plc
50 Bedford Square
London WC1B 3DP
www.bloomsbury.com

First edition 2014

Copyright © 2014 Paul Moore

ISBN (print): 978-1-4081-8223-9
ISBN (ePdf): 978-1- 4729-0050-0
ISBN (EPUB): 978-1-4729-0051-7

A CIP catalogue record for this book is available from the British Library.

Acknowledgements
Cover photographs © Getty Images
Inside photographs, see page 173

Commissioning editor Charlotte Croft
Original design Austin Taylor
Desk editor Nick Ascroft

This book is produced using paper that is made from wood grown in managed, sustainable forests. It is natural, renewable and recyclable. The logging and manufacturing processes conform to the environmental regulations of the country of origin.

Typeset in Scala Sans by seagulls.net

Printed and bound in China by C&C Offset Printing Co

10 9 8 7 6 5 4 3 2 1

CONTENTS

TO MY FAMILY. ALWAYS THERE.

Acknowledgements

First and foremost I would like to thank the athletes who gave up their time to help make this book happen. None of this would have been possible without them.

I would also like to thank my family for their unwavering support, continuous encouragement and an endless ability to listen. I could not have done this without you. The same thanks goes to Eva, whose patience apparently knows no bounds. Thank you for supporting me during the 3 a.m. interviews, for sitting through endless breakfasts/lunches/dinners and cups of tea as I floated thoughts around, and for always being there and always smiling. And thank you to my friends – my other 'family' – for their ideas, encouragement, and places to lay my head. Finally, I would like to thank my publishers, in particular Charlotte and Nick, for their patience and belief in this project.

About the *athletes*

THE FOLLOWING IS A SHORT PROFILE OF THE ATHLETES WHO ARE FEATURED IN THIS BOOK. ALL OF THEM HAVE BEEN WORLD CHAMPIONS, WORLD RECORD HOLDERS OR HOLD WORLD FIRSTS. THEY ARE A TRULY REMARKABLE GROUP OF INDIVIDUALS.

Craig ALEXANDER

Sport Ironman triathlon (3.9km swim, 180km bike, 42.2km run)

Achievements Ironman World Champion (2008, 2009, 2011); Ironman 70.3 World Champion (2006, 2011)

Website craigalexander.net

Craig Alexander is one of the greatest athletes in the history of Ironman triathlon. A five-time world champion, in 2011 Alexander became the first man to win both the Ironman 70.3 World Championships (in Las Vegas) and Ironman World Championships (in Kona, Hawaii) in the same year. He also holds the course record at the Ironman World Championships, crossing the line in 8 hours, 3 minutes and 56 seconds in 2011 (broken down into a 51:56 swim, 4:24:05 bike and 2:44:03 marathon).

Rachael CADMAN

Sport Triathlon

Achievements First woman to complete Enduroman Arch to Arc Triathlon (87-mile run, 22-mile swim, 181-mile bike)

Full-time RAF training officer and part-time triathlete, Rachael Cadman became the first woman – and only the eighth person – to complete the Enduroman Arch to Arc in 2011. Cadman completed the 87-mile run from Marble Arch in London to Dover on the south coast of England in 23 hours, 21 minutes and 8 seconds. She then swam the English Channel (approximately 22 miles but tide dependent) in 16 hours and 33 minutes, before cycling from Calais to the Arc de Triomphe in 20 hours and 16 minutes. She completed the race in 97 hours and 37 minutes.

Dee CAFFARI

Sport Sailing

Achievements First woman to circumnavigate the globe solo in a westerly direction (2006); First woman to circumnavigate the globe solo in both directions (2009)

Website deecaffari.co.uk

Dee Caffari sailed into the history books when in 2006 – after 178 days at sea – she completed a westerly solo circumnavigation of the globe. The westerly route sails against the prevailing winds and currents, and Caffari was the first woman to complete the voyage. Caffari then took on the challenge of becoming the first woman to circumnavigate the globe solo in both directions in 2009, when she finished sixth in the 2008/9 Vendée Globe. She has since completed one more circumnavigation (with a co-skipper) and currently holds the record for the fastest circumnavigation of Britain and Ireland (6 days, 11 hours, 30 minutes and 53 seconds).

Mirinda CARFRAE

Sport Ironman Triathlon (3.9km swim, 180km bike, 42.2km run)

Achievements Ironman World Champion (2010, 2013); Ironman 70.3 World Champion (2007); Runner-Up Ironman World Championships (2009, 2011)

Website mirindacarfrae.com

A latecomer to the world of triathlon, one year after taking part in her first race Mirinda Carfrae was selected for the Australian Junior Elite Team. A successful short-course career was followed by a stellar long-distance triathlon career that has seen Mirinda secure a raft of Ironman 70.3 victories around the world – including the world championship in a record time in 2007. However, the highlight of the Aussie's career came at the Hawaii Ironman World Championships, where Carfrae won the race at her second attempt. She won the race again in 2013, breaking the course record.

Mike HALL

Sport Cycling (multi-discipline)

Achievements World record holder for cycling round the world (18,000 miles)

Website normallyaspiratedhuman. com

After completing the 2,700-mile Tour Divide (from Canada to Mexico), Mike Hall was looking for a longer challenge. He found the longest: an 18,000-mile (minimum) circumnavigation of the globe. Mike set off with ten other riders from Greenwich, London as part of the World Cycle Racing Grand Tour: 91 days and 18 hours later, Hall was back in Greenwich having smashed the previous world record of 106 days, 10 hours and 33 minutes. Hall had averaged around 200 miles a day on his route through Europe to Turkey, across India, through Australia, New Zealand and the USA before returning to Europe and cycling up to the UK from Portugal.

George HINCAPIE

Sport Cycling (road)

Achievements Tour de France stage winner (2005); Tour Team Time Trial winner (2002, 2003, 2005); *Domestique* in Alberto Contador (2007) and Cadel Evans's (2011) Tour de France winning teams.

Website georgehincapie.com

One of the most respected road cyclists of his generation, George Hincapie led the peloton on to the Champs-Élysées to complete his seventeenth – and final – Tour de France in 2012. During a 19-year career, Hincapie forged a reputation as one of the greatest *domestiques* in the history of the sport. He was the only rider to compete with Lance Armstrong in every one of his now erased seven Tour de France 'wins'. He then went on to play a pivotal role in Alberto Contador and Cadel Evans's victories in 2007 and 2011 respectively. After announcing his retirement, Hincapie was one of a group of athletes who admitted to doping during the period that he rode with Armstrong on the US Postal Team.

Dean KARNAZES

Sport Ultra-marathon

Achievements Ran across America (3,000 miles); Ran 350 miles without stopping; 50 marathons in 50 States; Badwater Ultramarathon winner

Website ultramarathonman.com/web

After an epiphany on his thirtieth birthday, Dean Karnazes made the transition from corporate man to Ultra-marathon Man in a short space of time. Since turning his focus to ultra-marathon, Karnazes has won the Badwater Ultramarathon (2004), the Vermont Trail 100-Mile Endurance Run, and has competed at numerous high-profile endurance runs throughout the world. However, he is best known for the considerable challenges that he has set himself, which include: running 3,000 miles across the USA in 75 days; running 350 miles non-stop, completing 50 marathons in the 50 states of the USA in 50 days, and completing a marathon to the South Pole. As well as running, Karnazes has forged a successful career as an author and motivational speaker.

Rendy Lynn OPDYCKE

Sport Swimmer

Achievements Outright winner: Manhattan Island Marathon Swim (2006); record holder for the fastest completion of the Triple Crown of Open Water Swimming (English Channel, Manhattan Island Marathon Swim, Catalina Channel)

Rendy Lynn Opdycke has conquered the majority of the world's major ultra-swimming challenges. Among others, in 2004 she finished second (first woman) at the 28.5-mile Manhattan Island Marathon Swim (a swim around the island). She went one better in 2006 and won the race outright with the biggest margin of victory in the history of the event. In 2008, Opdycke broke the record for the fastest overall completion of the Triple Crown of Open Water Swimming, completing the Manhattan Island Marathon Swim in 7 hours, 46 minutes and 32 seconds, swimming the English Channel in 10 hours and 54 minutes and crossing California's Catalina Channel in 8 hours, 28 minutes and 21 seconds.

Stephen ROCHE

Sport Cycling (road)

Achievements 1987 Tour de France winner; 1987 Giro d'Italia winner; 1987 UCI Road World Championships winner (one of only two men to hold the Triple Crown of Cycling).

Website stephenroche.com

Stephen Roche boasted 58 wins in a professional cycling career that spanned 13 years. But he will always be remembered for one year of his career: 1987. In that year Roche achieved something that only one man, Eddy Merckx, had done before him: win the Triple Crown of Cycling. Over the course of four gruelling months, Roche won the Giro d'Italia, Tour de France and the Road World Championships. Roche carved out an impressive reputation with an unremitting will to win, riding himself into unconsciousness on one famous stage of the 1987 Tour de France.

Ryan SANDES

Sport Ultra-marathon

Achievements Winner: Leadville Trail 100; all four of the 4 Deserts ultra-marathons; the Jungle Marathon (new course record); North Face 100, Australia

Website ryansandes.com

After 'discovering' running relatively late in his life, Ryan Sandes has blazed a trail through the ultra-marathon world. After winning his first ultra-marathon (the 2008 Gobi March), Sandes went on to become the first – and only – person to win all four of the 4 Deserts ultra-marathon series of races (winning in the Gobi, Sahara, Atacama and Antarctica). Sandes has also tasted success at the infamous Leadville 100-mile trail run and the North Face 100 in Australia, as well as breaking records in Hong Kong, Brazil and on the Fish River Canyon Trail in Namibia.

Nicola SPIRIG

Sport Triathlon

Achievements Gold medal, London 2012 Olympic Games; European Champion (2009, 2010, 2012)

Website nicolaspirig.ch

Despite carving out a formidable reputation for herself in the ITU World Championship Series, the defining moment in Nicola Spirig's career was undoubtedly her win at the London 2012 Olympics. Spirig was awarded the win after a photo finish with Sweden's Lisa Nordén (the pair recorded identical finishing times). Spirig has won multiple races at ITU World Championship level and finished second in the 2010 World Championship series, and is three-time European Champion (2009, 2010 and 2012 – she was injured in 2011).

Brett SUTTON

Sport Triathlon (Coach)

Achievements Coached Chrissie Wellington to three Ironman World Championships; Nicola Spirig to Olympic Gold (London 2012); Emma Snowsill to Olympic Gold (Beijing 2008)

A formidable coach with an equally formidable reputation, Brett Sutton has trained some of the best triathletes in the history of the sport. Renowned for his unflinching, pragmatic approach to training, Sutton oversaw Chrissie Wellington's transition from leading amateur triathlete to three-time Ironman world champion. His squad boasts numerous Ironman champions, and he recently secured 'his' second Olympic Gold medal, coaching London 2012 Olympics winner Nicola Spirig, as well as 2008 Beijing Gold medallist Emma Snowsill. He has also coached numerous ITU (short-course) champions.

William TRUBRIDGE

Sport Freediving

Achievements World Record Holder: Constant Weight Without Fins (101 metres); Free Immersion (121 metres)

Website williamtrubridge.com

In 2010 William Trubridge became the first man to swim below 100 metres in the Constant Weight Without Fins discipline of freediving. Considered the purest form of diving, Constant Weight Without Fins means that the diver uses neither fins nor a rope and so must propel their bodies down – and back up – completely unassisted. He also broke the Free Immersion world record (where the diver can pull on a rope) in 2011, reaching 121 metres. In 2011 Trubridge won the World's Absolute Freediver Award. Operating out of the Bahamas, he is an apnea instructor at Vertical Blue, located at Dean's Blue Hole.

Todd WELLS

Sport Cycling (mountain bike, cyclo-cross)

Achievements Winner: Leadville Trail 100; La Ruta de los Conquistadores; USA Cyclo-cross and Cross Country National Championships; three-time Olympian.

Website toddwells.com

In 2010 Todd Wells became the first American to win the USA Cycling National Championships in three different disciplines: cyclo-cross, short track mountain biking and cross-country mountain biking. It was just a prelude for what was to come. In 2011 Wells secured his biggest wins, taking both the Leadville Trail 100 and the infamous La Ruta de los Conquistadores – a race across Costa Rica. In the summer of 2012 Wells competed in his third Olympic Games, finishing tenth in cross-country mountain biking (the highest finish for an American athlete at any Olympics).

INTRODUCTION

ENDURANCE SPORTS ATTRACT A RARE BREED OF ATHLETE. THEY ARE
INDIVIDUALS WHO NOT ONLY EMBRACE PAIN, BUT ALSO THRIVE ON IT.
THE BEST ENDURANCE ATHLETES CAN PUSH THEIR BODIES FURTHER,
HARDER – AND OFTEN FASTER – THAN CONVENTIONAL NORM DICTATES
POSSIBLE. AND ONCE THE PAIN SUBSIDES AND THE ACHING FADES AWAY,
THESE ATHLETES COME BACK FOR MORE.

Making the **commitment**

To be an endurance athlete you have to suffer, you have to sacrifice, and you have to struggle. That is the nature of the pursuit. But to overcome the challenge there is one thing that is as important as superb physical conditioning, and that is mental strength. Whatever the sport and its overall goal, it is ultimately your mind that urges you to place one foot in front of the other after hours of racing. And so whether you finish first or fiftieth, or even finish at all, your mind, in connection with your body, is vital in getting you there.

The journey to the finish line of an endurance event is long and hard. It begins with your decision to commit to that event, then progresses along a road of training and preparation, and finishes when you have recovered enough to evaluate the success (or lack thereof) in realising the goals that you have established along the way.

Taking that first step – committing to an event or a challenge – is one of the hardest parts of that journey. By making that commitment you are doing more than simply paying the (sometimes quite considerable) entry fee for an event. You are committing your time and energy to the pursuit of a difficult goal. Realising that goal will take focus. What's more, it will demand sacrifice.

To start with, social relationships will undoubtedly change. Ultra-marathon runner Dean Karnazes discovered that when he made the transition from corporate executive to full-time endurance athlete:

❝ What we do is very polarising; people either get it or they don't. Some people either relate to that brazen and bold mindset of saying: 'Hey, I'm going to do what I love and push my body and that's my thing – exploring the limits of human endurance – I'm going to do it.' Other people don't. Ultimately I gained a lot of new friends and became closer with some of my distant friends, but I also lost a lot of my friends because my interests were moving in a different direction to theirs. So it changed the posse I hung out with.

More than social relationships, though, pursuing endurance sports places significant demands on family relationships. Even professional athletes experience periods when they rue the sheer time and effort required to realise their goals. Three-time Ironman World Champion Craig Alexander finds this aspect of his sport the hardest part of the profession.

❝ **The toughest thing** for me has been wanting to spend a lot of time with the kids when I have to go out training. Or wanting to watch my daughter's soccer games or swim meets or that kind of thing. I have been able to do that – to find a nice balance so that I don't feel guilty about leaving the kids.

But essentially, this is still my job and I'm lucky I've got a very supportive wife and with time management she makes sure I don't miss out on anything. That makes me happy and I think that when you're in an emotionally good place your training is much better.

Relationships aren't the only thing that endurance athletes sacrifice. There are plenty of personal sacrifices to be made too. There is the fatigue –

and its associated impact – that accompanies the months of training and racing. Then there are the smaller things, like diet. If you speak to enough endurance athletes they will invariably talk about their racing weight. That involves – and there are entire books dedicated to this – hitting the ideal power-to-weight ratio in a bid to maximise performance. Every serious endurance athlete – pro and amateur alike – knows about racing weights, and many choose dietary sacrifices to realise that weight. Three-time Olympian and 2011 La Ruta de los Conquistadores champion Todd Wells has learnt to incorporate this as part of a rigorous mountain-bike regimen. In fact, it's one of the things he finds toughest about his sport.

❝ **Definitely the eating**. I like to eat and it's not that I'm a super skinny guy – I'm 6 foot 2 and weigh around 170 pounds – I could train all I wanted to, but if I ate what I wanted then I would probably weigh 190 pounds.

But if sacrifice lies at the heart of the endurance sport experience, then it does so beside reward.

Athletes who have committed to endurance sports acknowledge that they have had to change aspects of their lives and sacrifice certain things and, at times, certain people. But they also tell of the immense benefits that competing in endurance sports afford them, from travelling to parts of the world that few people ever get to see, to the sense of satisfaction at overcoming a truly formidable challenge. The rewards are varied and plentiful. There is, however, one benefit to competing in endurance sports that stands out for each and every athlete who pushes themselves to their physical and mental limits: self-discovery. 'It's a test of your endurance but also of your mental strength,' says ultra-marathon runner Ryan Sandes. 'I think you learn a hell of a lot about yourself when you're running 100 miles and things aren't going your way. You learn a lot about both yourself and what you're made of.'

Endurance sports are not just physically demanding. They teach individuals about themselves – both as an athlete and as a person. Very few people walk away from endurance sports without having learnt a lesson about what they are capable of or how they are able to overcome physical or mental adversity. To that extent alone, endurance sports are rewarding.

They are also fun. We look at the motivation behind endurance events in more detail in Chapter 2 (Motivation: Keeping the fire burning). However, one of the reasons why you are thinking about committing to an endurance event is because you enjoy swimming, running, rowing, cycling, climbing or another sport that you recognise will push your physical and mental limits. Endurance sports simply give people more time and more reasons to participate in that sport. What's more, by the end of the journey you will be stronger and better at your chosen sport. There is an enormous sense of satisfaction at having realised that sort of personal development in a pastime.

Most athletes who commit to endurance events (particularly in the early stages of their 'careers') focus purely on their physical development. However, having made that commitment it is equally as important to develop the right mental attitude towards these sports. It is ultimately the mind that drives the body. Of course, training plays a huge role in toughening up the mind and giving the

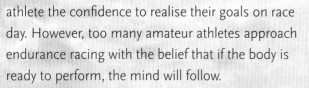

athlete the confidence to realise their goals on race day. However, too many amateur athletes approach endurance racing with the belief that if the body is ready to perform, the mind will follow.

In reality, it is often the other way round.

There are numerous discussions about the link between thoughts, emotions and physical performance. Indeed, listen to enough professional athletes and they will talk about races where they either 'felt ready' or they just 'weren't there'. The way an athlete feels and thinks ahead of a race will directly impact the way they perform, regardless of how much training they have done. That is why so many professional athletes spend significant periods of their time working on their mental strength. They do so to give themselves the best opportunity of realising their goals on race day.

That is what this book is about: developing the right mental attitude for endurance performance. We begin from the premise that the athlete who is prepared to develop their mental approach to sport will not only give a stronger performance, but

stands a better chance of achieving their goals. With the help of some of the world's best athletes, this book examines numerous ways that athletes can develop their mental strength. Not every method will be applicable to every athlete – we are all individuals and, like our training programmes, there is no one-size-fits-all solution to developing mental strength. However, the ideas, concepts and case studies presented in this book will, hopefully, give you a better understanding of how the mind of an athlete works, and the various elements of that mind that need to be managed to realise the optimum endurance performance.

If you commit to an endurance event you have to do so accepting that you will encounter hard times. What's more, there will probably be times when you feel like giving up. Don't. Those are the times that define the endurance sports experience. They are also the key moments that will see you push your own personal boundaries and amaze yourself at what you are capable of. That knowledge is the ultimate reward afforded to all endurance athletes, and makes all of the sacrifices entirely worthwhile.

1

What is mental toughness?

Sport is littered with stories and examples of mental toughness. Every keen observer of sport can recall a time when they have watched the performance of a sportsman or woman implode in the heat of 'the moment'. Similarly, they can remember a time when an athlete has stood firm. When, in the face of pressure or extreme physical fatigue, an individual has been able to overcome adversity and realise their goals. These are the athletes who are revered. Who are winners. Who are said to be mentally tough.

But despite the repeated references to mental toughness in sport, what does that term actually mean? Of course, it means that someone is mentally strong. But mental strength and mental toughness are fundamentally the same things. What's more, they are essentially ethereal concepts. How are they defined and how are they measured? Answering – or at least attempting to answer – those questions is the perfect place to begin a book about endurance performance.

The psychologists' *perspective*

Sports psychology and the analysis of performance have witnessed a dramatic growth over the last decade or so. Of course, sport has always been an area of interest for psychologists. But as the industry of sport has evolved, the tools available to athletes to help them improve their performance have also become more advanced. Psychology is one of those tools. Techniques and strategies for strengthening the mind are abundant, and plenty of top-flight athletes employ the services of psychologists to help them manage their performance under pressure. As this field has developed, so too has the interest in defining what is widely seen to be one of the key determinants of sporting success: mental toughness.

While there have been numerous studies that have attempted to define mental toughness, two catch the eye in their pursuit of a thorough definition.

In a study that took place in 2002, Graham Jones at the University of Wales spoke to ten international athletes, all of whom had represented their country at a major event, from across the sporting spectrum. After a three-stage process that saw the athletes first interviewed and then completing

George **HINCAPIE**

❝ Mental toughness is a very important component of being a successful athlete or a successful person in life in general. It's just as important as training and nutrition and all of those elements.

this page Although very different characters, Usain Bolt (top), Roger Federer (bottom left) and Michael Phelps (bottom right) are famous for their ability to deal with pressure.

questionnaires, Jones was able to offer the following definition of mental toughness:

> " **Mental toughness** is having the natural or developed psychological edge that enables you to:
> - Generally, cope better than your opponents with the many demands (competition, training, lifestyle) that sport places on a performer.
> - Specifically, be more consistent and better than your opponents in remaining determined, focused, confident, and in control under pressure.

The interesting thing to note from Jones's definition of mental toughness is that both variables directly measure the performance of the athlete against that of their opponent. As a result, this definition creates a direct link between mental toughness and winning. In the context of mainstream sports, and with a mind to the popular determinants of success, the definition works perfectly. No athlete who has won a major event when competing against others has, from recollection, been defined as mentally weak. Indeed, the sportsmen and women who are revered in the mainstream press – the likes of Roger Federer, Michael Phelps or Usain Bolt – although very different personalities, are famous for their mental toughness and ability to channel that into their sport, and so defeat the opposition.

Endurance sports are, however, slightly different and so the definition does not sit so easily. Athletes who are competing professionally undoubtedly benchmark themselves and their success against their opponents (more on that later). However, there is a significant body of athletes competing at all levels of endurance sports who are not racing to defeat an opponent unless that opponent is time or distance. These athletes can still be defined as mentally tough. Even in professional endurance sports there are athletes who are more interested in challenging themselves physically rather than beating their opponents. In relation to these

---

left A determined Chris Froome dominated the 2013 Tour de France.

athletes – some of who complete challenges that demand exceptional levels of mental toughness – the Jones (2002) definition falls slightly short.

Middleton et. al. (2005) produced a slightly different interpretation of mental toughness in an entirely independent study from Jones. They interviewed 33 participants from across the sporting spectrum, 25 of whom had represented their country at international level. After multiple interviews, they were able to produce a preliminary definition of mental toughness as being:

> " **An unshakeable** perseverance and conviction towards some goal despite pressure or adversity.

Because this definition is decidedly more generalised, it fits perfectly within the framework of endurance sports. Endurance athletes often perform under pressure, and regularly do so against adversity. What's more, the dedication that endurance athletes display towards realising a goal or goals is absolute, to the point where even amateur endurance athletes structure their lives around their sport. By adopting this definition of mental toughness, we also remove the demands of winning, a demand that is only applicable at certain levels and in certain disciplines of endurance sports. As such, we begin to form a definition of mental strength that sits well against the demands of endurance performance.

The pros' *perspective*

Perhaps the reason why sports psychologists have produced different definitions of the same term is because sportsmen and women interpret mental toughness differently. As we will see in Chapter 2 (Motivation: Keeping the fire burning), athletes – regardless of whether they are professionals or amateurs – are motivated by many different things. For example, some are motivated by the challenge, some by the victory, and some by the pursuit of the perfect performance. While mental toughness undoubtedly plays a substantial role in them being able to realise their goals and maintain this motivation, it stands to reason that with different goals and motivations they will have different perspectives of what mental toughness is.

Pro-cyclist George Hincapie was not only renowned for his mental strength, but played an instrumental role in helping both Alberto Contador and Cadel Evans secure their Tour de France yellow jerseys. He was also the only man to ride with Lance Armstrong during every one of his now-erased seven Tour de France victories. His perspective on the role of mental toughness is clear.

> **Mental toughness** is a very important component of being a successful athlete or a successful person in life in general. It's just as important as training and nutrition and all of those elements.

Road cycling is a famously unforgiving sport. Over the course of a career that spanned 19 years, Hincapie forged a reputation as one of the best *domestiques* in the history of the sport. He played this role for numerous Tour de France champions (Hincapie rode in a record-equalling nine Tour-winning teams), and rode alongside some of the toughest athletes on the planet. In his mind, though, two cyclists stood out in terms of exhibiting supreme mental toughness.

> **I would say** either Lance [Armstrong] or Cadel [Evans]. In 2011, Cadel was on his own going up the Col du Galibier and Andy Schleck was riding away from him and he went to the front of a group in a headwind up a climb and basically limited all his damages and kept himself in a position to win the Tour – and he ended up winning it. To have that mental strength after three weeks of racing, that's a prime example.
>
> Lance, I've gone out on training rides with him when I was as fit as I've ever been and done a seven-hour ride with five mountains and we'd get to the top of Alpe d'Huez and Lance would say 'I'm going to do this one again.' For me that was an impossible thought because I was so exhausted and after a seven-hour ride you'd think 'why would you need to do that?'

But that was the kind of drive and determination that Lance has.

While Hincapie does not offer an outright definition of mental toughness, he provides examples that lend themselves to defining the term. Cadel Evans's ride up the Col du Galibier epitomised his unwavering drive towards the Tour de France title in 2011. Similarly, despite the revelations about his drug use, Lance Armstrong forged a formidable reputation for riding further and training harder than any other athlete in the peloton.

This need for determination is echoed by 2010 and 2013 Ironman world champion Mirinda Carfrae. Carfrae is widely renowned as being the fastest runner in Ironman triathlon and holds both the Kona course run record (2 hours, 50 minutes and 38 seconds) and overall Kona course record (8 hours, 52 minutes and 14 seconds). Like Hincapie, rather than define mental strength Carfrae instead relates it to her own experience:

> **I'm not really sure** what mental strength means. For me it's about racing in Kona and having to push for such a long period of time. But there are so many different aspects of being mentally strong. There are so many different obstacles throughout the year and throughout your life where you have to push back and be mentally strong. And certainly the image that encapsulates that is being out on the Queen K or the Energy Lab and pushing through what seems like hell.

Interestingly, neither Hincapie nor Carfrae offered definitions of mental toughness that benchmarked it against the need to win. That's not to say that they aren't motivated to win – both have done so at some of the biggest races in their respective sports – just that winning is not a necessary part of being mentally strong for them. However, there are athletes who see a direct relationship between mental strength and winning.

Swiss triathlete Nicola Spirig, who won Gold at the London 2012 Olympics, views it as the defining factor between victory and defeat:

above (From left to right) Craig Alexander, Chrissie Wellington and Mirinda Carfrae – three of the most talented Ironman triathletes of their generation.

❝ *I think mental strength* is really important in professional sports because at races like the Olympics or the Worlds there are athletes at the same level physically. Between those athletes mental strength will decide who wins.

As detailed in Chapter 14 (When it all comes together), Spirig was awarded the Gold medal at the London 2012 Olympics after a photo finish with Sweden's Lisa Nordén. Timing chips could not separate the pair. When she reflects on that race, she puts her victory down to her will to win. Brett Sutton, her coach, believes that that will to win is a direct result of Spirig's mental toughness.

❝ *I just think* she was so mentally strong and had confidence in herself.

This link between winning and mental toughness is also one Stephen Roche agrees with. Roche, who famously completed the Triple Crown of Cycling in 1987 by winning the Giro d'Italia, Tour de France and World Championships in one year, has a very clear view on what mental toughness is:

❝ **Not being happy** with second. Mental strength is when you look at someone who is climbing a hill and they're pulling faces you think 'I'm getting it tough but he's getting it even worse' and that's mental toughness. When you can look across at the guy across from you and say 'I'm suffering but he is too.'

But also being in the negative situation – the Tour could be over for you or the race could be over for you – and all of a sudden you could be reacting and going into overdrive. On the climbs when you're getting it really hard it's being able to dig in, think about the win and all the hard work you've put into it and being very

above Mountain biker Todd Wells takes a tumble

tough on yourself and not hammering yourself because you won or you came second. To me it's win. It's not about numbers, it's about winning. End of story.

Like psychologists, professional athletes are divided between whether mental toughness is defined by winning or by the relentless pursuit of their goals. For many professional athletes, the two go hand in hand.

In reality, the meaning of mental toughness is different for each and every one of us. For many professional athletes mental toughness is the ability to defeat an opponent. In the context of sport as a whole it seems more apt to define it as the ability to realise predefined goals. In the specific instance of endurance sports it is widely perceived as being the ability to push on through when times are hard.

As such, the definition of mental toughness has to reflect all of these interpretations. Throughout this book we will refer to mental toughness on a regular basis. In so doing we are primarily referencing an athlete's ability to overcome adversity and pressure. In many respects that ability is the essence of endurance sports, and what many people think of when they try to define endurance athletes.

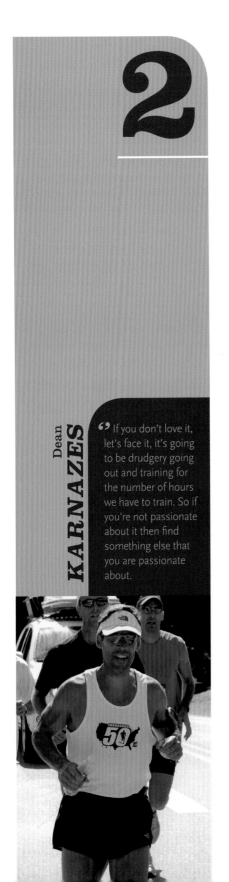

2

Motivation:
Keeping the fire burning

Why are you doing this? When you sign up for an endurance event you have to be prepared to answer that question. What's more, it's not just a question that will be levelled at you by friends, colleagues or family. Rather, it is one that you will probably ask yourself on more than one occasion. And while you can fob other people off with reasons and excuses, it is not so easy to do that to yourself. So, why are you doing this?

Motivation comes in all shapes and sizes. However, when you really drill down into it, it has two basic forms: intrinsic motivation and extrinsic motivation.

Intrinsic factors are those that are personal to the individual. They are based on interests and drive. For instance, an athlete might choose to run a marathon or ultra-marathon because they love running and have a very real interest in seeing how their body performs over long distances. Another athlete may spend more time swimming because they have an interest in mastering the technical aspects of the sport. Alternatively, an athlete may choose to take on an Ironman because it is hard, and they have a real desire to challenge themselves and overcome that challenge.

Extrinsic factors are entirely different. Rather than being driven by personal interest, the athlete is instead motivated by reward. In endurance sports the most common extrinsic factor that motivates athletes is the desire to earn respect or praise from other people. However, in mainstream sports, particularly at the professional end, extrinsic motivational factors can be financial, the development of fame/celebrity or the winning of trophies/awards.

Of course, there is nothing wrong with being motivated by extrinsic factors. In fact, in any professional sports, extrinsic factors are generally associated with success, and many athletes and sportsmen are motivated by them. However, it is almost impossible to reach that high level of professionalism in sport – or any endeavour, for that matter – being solely motivated by extrinsic factors.

Extrinsic factors are less of a feature in high-level endurance sports than other sporting pursuits for many reasons. First and foremost, as Dean Karnazes explains, 'There is no prize money in these events. If I win the Badwater Ultramarathon I get a belt buckle like everyone else.' With the notable exception of road cycling, only a few professional endurance athletes will take home an above national-average income from competing in their sport alone. What's more, with the mainstream media taking a limited interest in many endurance events throughout the year, the cultivation of celebrity can also be ruled out as a key-motivating factor (again, road cycling is a notable exception). Of course, one key extrinsic factor that drives many endurance athletes is winning, success and the accumulation of awards. However, as we discuss later in this chapter, that is part and parcel of the basic nature of sporting competition.

With this in mind it makes sense to examine the intrinsic factors that motivate athletes. Needless to say, the motivational factors that drive many of the athletes featured in *Ultra Performance* will become clearer from their various observations during the course of this book. This chapter, though, looks at the specifics of motivation away from extrinsic factors and towards those intrinsic factors that motivate the athletes to train and ultimately to perform. They are the factors that lie at the heart of athletic performance, and they are the factors that drive already successful athletes to continue competing. In many respects, these intrinsic factors are not entirely different from those that spur you or me. Maybe at times they are at a different intensity or executed at a different level. But at their core they are the basic drive that pushes every athlete who chooses to tackle endurance events.

Motivation and the *athlete*

It is very difficult to be a successful endurance athlete – at any level – without enjoying what you do. There's a simple reason for that, as explained by road-cycling legend George Hincapie:

> ❝ **You can't do cycling** half-arsed, you have to be all in or it's not worth it. The pain is too much.

Whatever your chosen endurance pursuit, the training will be hard. And at times it will be unpleasant. As a result, athletes share one common intrinsic motivation: 'Passion.

You have to be passionate about what you do and you have to love it,' says ultra-marathon runner Dean Karnazes.

> ❝ **If you don't love it,** let's face it, it's going to be drudgery going out and training for the number of hours we have to train. So if you're not passionate about it then find something else that you are passionate about.

Karnazes's view on the importance of passion is shared by many of his contemporaries. Fellow ultra-marathon runner Ryan Sandes believes that his success is bred from his love of running.

> ❝ **You've got to enjoy** what you do. I think the reason I have been successful is because I'm super passionate about what I do and I really enjoy it. I always say that if you're doing something and you don't enjoy it then half the time you're not going to be successful so try and find something you really enjoy doing.

Whatever the level the athlete performs at, passion, and the enjoyment of a chosen sport, has to be the central factor that motivates him or her. Endurance sports are too hard and require too much physical and mental dedication to be pursued if the individual does not enjoy what they do. Of course, there will be times when motivation temporarily wanes or when the athlete experiences a dip in form and a correlating reduction in performance. But it is a solid, basic presumption that the athlete will continue to pursue their chosen sport regardless, simply because they enjoy doing it.

It is perfectly normal for an athlete to enjoy training for a sport but not want to compete over significant distances. For instance, there are plenty of club cyclists around the world who choose not to cycle for five hours per day. The same with runners. These athletes take enjoyment from their pastime without dedicating significant volumes of time and energy to that pursuit.

Endurance athletes are slightly different, though. They are not only motivated by the sport, but by the challenge that their sport affords them. As Sandes puts it:

above Endurance sports are too hard
not to enjoy doing what you do.

❝ *I think for me* it's always about setting myself new challenges. In the beginning it was completing the 4 Deserts or a couple of the multi-day races – that's how I got into ultra-running. But then a lot of people said: 'Why don't you continue doing the 4 Deserts series?' I think I would have grown bored and probably wouldn't have been as driven or focused if I had continued to do the same thing. So at the moment I'm focusing on the classic 100-mile races like Leadville, Western States or UTMB and a couple of the 100km races around the world. The goal going forward is to get as close as possible to the top of the podium for both of them.

below Ultra marathon races take place in some of the toughest parts of the world.

If I get that right then I would have to reassess things. But I definitely think that being able to perform at that level you definitely need challenges and ambitions and dreams, so maybe I would have to find another sport if I found it becoming too easy.

Sandes is referring to goals that he has set himself for specific races. However, some of the world's top endurance athletes, Sandes included, are motivated by more than just the challenge of individual races. They are motivated by the challenge of perceived physical boundaries. They are quite simply looking to see how far or hard they can go.

'There's a quote that I live by: "impossible is just a word" and I think that it's true,' says Rendy Lynn Opdycke. Opdycke has a remarkable résumé for an

endurance athlete who is still at a relatively early stage of her career. As well as winning the 28-mile Manhattan Island Marathon Swim outright (with the biggest margin of victory in the history of the race), the American also holds the record for the fastest completion of the Triple Crown of Swimming (the Manhattan Island Marathon Swim, English Channel and Catalina Channel swims) in the shortest time possible. An immense physical, mental and logistical challenge, Opdycke completed all three swims in a 35-day period during the summer of 2008.

❝ If you put your mind to it and you put your guts to it, you can pretty much do anything.

below Open water swimming is a true test of mental and physical strength.

This drive to push physical boundaries is a common motivational thread for the world's best endurance athletes. Of course, all of these physical boundaries are relative and it is up to the athletes to determine where their limits lie.

Every single one of the athletes featured in this book made calculated decisions when exploring how far or how hard they should go. They push their boundaries in incremental stages, exploring the limits of their physical abilities. And they also realise when they have reached those limits. Dean Karnazes is a case in point. The American runner has made a considerable name for himself by completing some quite extraordinary physical challenges during the course of his running career. The motivation for these challenges? To discover his own limits:

“ ***My attitude is*** best summed up by the saying: 'never stop exploring'. The idea of continually pushing yourself and seeking greater and greater challenges, that is my passion. Once I did a 50-mile race I thought 'My God, I've just run 50 miles' and then I heard about a 100-mile race and I thought 'How can a human being run 100 miles without stopping? That's incredible, that's absurd, I've got to try it.' So then I ran 100 miles and then I heard about this 135-mile race across Death Valley and I kept thinking 'Gosh, how far can I go?'

Back then there was really no organised foot race – a single person, single stage race – that was beyond 135 miles. That was the furthest there was. But then I learnt about this 200-mile relay race – a 12-person relay race – and I thought 'I wonder if I could do the whole thing myself?' so I talked to the race director and convinced him to let me do it and I ran 200 miles. And I thought: 'My God, I just ran 200 miles non-stop in under 48 hours' and I wondered if I could go further than that. So I then wondered if I could run ten marathons back to back – 262 miles – without stopping. So the next year in the 200-mile race I ran 100km – 62 miles – to the start line and got there and started the race and I was able to run 262 miles and I thought 'I wonder how much further I can go?' and I set my sights on 350 miles, and so 200 of those 350 were part of this relay race. I thought that maybe a human being could run 500 miles without stopping. But 350 miles to me was psychotic.

I'm not a super spiritual guy but I would say that I had an out-of-body experience in that run. There was a point on the third night without sleep – I think I was at about mile 318 – and all of a sudden I was looking down upon a guy running. Literally in my mind's eye that was where I was. Even though I was on the ground running I was looking down at the guy running as though I was in a helicopter but then I realised 'Oh my God, the guy that's down there, that's me.' And I thought that maybe that was what you see right before you die!

opposite 'I am discovering what my body is capable of doing' – William Trubridge

There is an extremely limited number of people who would be physically capable of running 350 miles without stopping. What's more, there are probably even fewer people who would be motivated to do so. Karnazes found his motivation in his own desire to explore his physical limits. What's more, he knew when to stop.

World-record-holding freediver William Trubridge is also motivated by the desire to discover his physical limits. In doing so, Trubridge is also defining the limits of human endurance. In December 2010 Trubridge became the first human being to dive to a depth of 100 metres completely unassisted. He then broke his own world record two days later, reaching 101 metres. Freediving is a sport where divers can use rope, weights and mechanical sleds to help them achieve some quite startling depths. Trubridge, however, generally competes in the Constant Weight Without Fins freediving discipline, where the diver swims down and back completely unassisted (no fins, rope or other equipment). It is generally considered to be the purest form of freediving. Trubridge has repeatedly broken his own world records in this discipline, but remains motivated to keep on pushing the known physical limits of human underwater endurance:

“ ***I guess for me*** it's less about the world records – they are still important and I get a buzz from breaking them – but it's more about the process of discovery and exploration and feeling like I am discovering what my body is capable of doing and what we as human beings are capable of doing under water.

The thrill of that exploration is the greatest motivation. As long as I have that I think I will continue freediving (as well as that the pleasure of being underwater, being at depth and the tranquillity of it). It's the otherworldly nature of being under the water. If I was motivated by world records I might be satisfied with what I have at the moment and maybe lose motivation because I have achieved that goal. Likewise, if I wasn't able to break world records I would get disheartened by that and leave the sport. But because

above 'The perfect performance may be an illusion, but it's the pursuit of that that interests me' – Craig Alexander

opposite For cycling time trials you are alone with your race plan and the limits of your resources.

those aren't my main motivations there is no danger that I will stop freediving because of it.

The world of Ironman triathlon is a million miles away from the underwater exploits of William Trubridge. However, the motivation that drives Trubridge is not entirely dissimilar to that which pushes three-time Ironman World Champion Craig Alexander to keep competing. Alexander is a ferocious competitor and, as we discuss in Chapter 13 (Winning: It's all in the mind), has repeatedly demonstrated his almost unrivalled passion for competition. But the thrill of competing – and indeed dominating – Ironman triathlon is not what motivates Alexander. Rather, a little bit like Trubridge, it is the pursuit of sustained improvements in exceptional performance – seeing what his body is capable of – that drives the Australian:

❝ **For me it's not** about breaking records or winning more Kona titles than anyone else, it's about improving every year. That's where the motivation comes from, it's very simple. That, and being a better athlete. There are always things that you can do in a sport like Ironman to improve.

Obviously the steep part of the improvement curve is long gone but you're looking for the one percenters as the football coaches call them – the little half-percentage increments here and there. At the highest level of any sport it is usually a big investment of time and effort and energy to get little incremental improvements but that's what you're after and it's exciting when you see those improvements.

It's funny, when I won in Kona in 2011 I was the oldest man to ever win and everyone kept reminding me of that in every interview. That's fine – it's inevitable when you get to your mid- to late-thirties the question of retirement comes up. And it's a fair question. How long can you keep going? People tend to want to make excuses for you or they want to make it easy for you: 'you've got nothing left to prove', 'what more could you want to achieve?' and I also heard 'what a great way

to go out'. And I thought: 'what a great way to go out but also what a great way to continue'. What's left to achieve? What's left to achieve is what has always been there to achieve: being the best athlete that I could be. And let's be honest, the perfect performance may be an ideal or an illusion but it's the pursuit of that that interests me. Whatever the perfect performance is to where I am now, I'm sure there's space between that in the interim somewhere there and that's what I'm interested in: tapping into that.

When Michael Johnson was ruling the world at 200 and 400 metres one of the tools he used to maintain his motivation was clearing out the trophy cabinet at the end of a year and starting each season from zero. Craig Alexander adopts a similar approach, choosing to ignore the trophies and awards – the extrinsic motivators – and focusing instead on his pursuit of perfection.

> *I have a short memory* like that. I'm not really interested in looking back and admiring what's on the mantelpiece other than from the perspective of trying to learn from the performance. I'll admire all of that when my career is over. To me the challenge is improving every year across the board in all aspects of my racing and training and preparation.

The athletes profiled throughout this book have achieved some quite remarkable things. Many are – or have been – world champions, many have realised world firsts or world records, all have carved out considerable reputations for achieving quite remarkable things in their respective sports. And while the thought of dominating their sport has undoubtedly helped to motivate them, it is the intrinsic factors that have helped to push them further, faster or harder. So while many professional athletes are capable of achieving things that most normal people simply cannot, the things that motivate them to push their bodies to realise these goals are the same things that motivate you or I to get up in the morning and train. As athletes they enjoy the challenge, they enjoy

pushing their boundaries, and they enjoy working hard to perfect their sport. But above all of that, they enjoy what they do. They are motivated to compete by the sport itself, and they are passionate about that sport. In that respect, professional endurance athletes are no different to Saturday morning cyclists or the masters' session swimmers. Of course, for the most part they go faster having had more time to hone their performance. But they have done that because that is what they want to do. That is their passion.

This chapter began by asking you why you wanted to take part in an endurance event. The reason that question was posed was because you need to know this in order to successfully tackle the issues we deal with in the next two chapters. The first of these is goal setting – something that is inherently tied into motivation. The second is training. Arguably harder than the race itself, managing training – and in particular training volumes – is one of the toughest aspects of being an endurance athlete. And whether you are a pro athlete or a first-timer, training is something that we cannot escape from.

MOTIVATION: KEY POINTS

- Motivation comes in two forms: intrinsic (personal rewards) and extrinsic (financial, ego rewards). Endurance athletes are generally motivated by intrinsic factors.
- Passion – or at least real enjoyment of your sport – is essential for a long endurance career.
- There will be times of challenge and of suffering. You have to be willing to accept these to push your limits.
- A focus on the process (e.g. technique, implementation of race strategy etc.) is more important than focusing on the outcome (e.g. winning).

3

Goal setting:
Taking aim at the target

Once you have made the commitment to pursuing your chosen sport, the next step is to establish goals. Pursuing a goal is, after all, the driving force behind that original commitment. Some athletes set an initial goal of simply aiming to finish. Then, as they progress in their sport, these goals may broaden to include working on particular aspects of their performance or realising specific time goals. At the elite end of the field these goals become even more specific: to win, to place top ten, to qualify for a championships or to hit specific numbers (time, power, etc.). All of these goals serve to motivate athletes to prepare for – and then to perform on – race day. On the surface, the process of establishing goals is relatively straightforward. An athlete commits to an event or series of events, establishes their targets at these events, and then starts training towards these targets. However, after an initial burst of enthusiasm, many endurance athletes struggle to maintain their focus on these goals, and very often the original target is missed or altered as fatigue kicks in and time ticks away.

However, with a bit of planning and thought, goals can be established that help you maintain motivation throughout the various phases of a training programme. These goals fall into three main groups: 'A' goals, 'B' goals and immediate goals.

Establishing 'A' *goals*

An athlete's 'A' goal should be a specific goal or goals targeting a specific race (or series of races). For the majority of non-professional endurance athletes these goals are time-orientated (for instance 'I am going to run X time at this marathon' or 'I will go sub-X at this Ironman') or focus on improvements in a specific part of the event ('I am going to negative split' or 'My bike will be X minutes faster than last year'). For these goals to be effective motivational tools, they have to be challenging, realistic and specific.

CHALLENGING

If you can swim 3 kilometres in one hour and two minutes then setting a goal of going sub-one hour in 12 months' time does not represent a significant challenge. However, going sub-50 is not only realistic but also challenging at the same time. Setting this kind of goal will not only motivate, but also will give you plenty to work on during the training phase.

REALISTIC

Very few athletes enter an endurance race and win at their first go. There are, of course, notable exceptions (Chrissie Wellington in Ironman and Ryan Sandes in ultra-marathon), but they are not the norm. As such, if you have never placed well (or even competed) in a cyclosportive, for instance, and you set a goal of winning a national stage race then there is a very real risk of overreaching and thus becoming demotivated during the training phase. If, however, you take a look at the results of that event in previous years and set your target on a placing based on these numbers, you can establish ambitious, achievable goals that will motivate you through the process. By all means, you should challenge yourself, but that challenge should be established with a view to both your ability and previous performances.

SPECIFIC

The more specific your goals are, the more chance you have of realising them. For a novice athlete to aim to complete a marathon in less than four hours is a specific goal. To try really hard to complete a marathon is not. This non-specificity will ultimately undermine the motivation of an athlete and could lead to easy excuses to miss sessions when the training get tough. If you have a specific target to aim for then you will be motivated to train towards this goal.

Establishing 'B' *goals*

'B' goals are the targets that you set along the way to help you build towards a performance in your 'A' goal (or goals). They are directly related to 'A' goals in that they will allow you to benchmark your development during the training phase. However, they are also valuable in

terms of motivation, giving you short- and medium-term objectives as you prepare for a race that could be months away. 'B' goals can be event- and training-specific:

EVENT-SPECIFIC GOALS

Athletes build up to races over periods of many months. Occasionally, the time taken to build towards an event can be quite demotivating. Entering shorter, tune-up races can provide you with an invaluable motivation and can also help you learn about aspects of your performance. You should enter these races with specific targets in mind. For instance, some athletes will target time, while others will target specific aspects of performance (see Rachael Cadman's perspective on build-up races in Chapter 4 – Training: Building confidence through preparation).

TRAINING-SPECIFIC GOALS

One of the common traps that many endurance athletes fall into is to focus on the volume of training as opposed to the quality of it. As you look to develop and progress your performance in a discipline or disciplines, you can set yourself time targets in training. For instance, completing a swim time trial in X minutes, running 10 kilometres in under X, etc. These targets will give you a specific training goal that will enable you to measure your progress as you build towards your 'A' goals.

Immediate *goals*

At the start of any training phase you need to evaluate your historical performances and identify areas that need work. Developing strategies and training plans that will allow you to focus on these areas are the immediate goals. These goals are generally process goals: they will help you develop aspects of your performance and

opposite Pound-for-pound one of the fastest men on two wheels: Mark Cavendish.

ultimately push you to realise a successful outcome. For instance, immediate goals can vary from working on specific aspects of technique to ensuring that training volumes are realised.

These goals are also progressive. Of course, you can focus on the original set of goals in the first weeks of training, but you should then mould and develop them as your training progresses, using them to improve specific aspects of performance as you build towards your 'B' goals and, ultimately, your 'A' goals. The key element with these goals is that they have a time frame to them.

TIME-SPECIFICITY

If you structure an immediate goal as 'I want to improve my swim stroke', not only is there a distinct lack of general specificity to it, but there is no time frame. If, however, your goal is structured as: 'I want to improve my swim

stroke and complete X time trial in six weeks' then you have a time frame in which to realise your objectives (and that will hopefully help them to do so).

Although we propose three levels of goal setting, you should not burden yourself by setting too many goals. The 'A' goal should focus on one (or perhaps two) primary objectives over the course of a season. The 'B' goals should be key points of the journey towards realising the 'A' goal, and the immediate goals should be process driven, working on the areas of performance that will allow you to realise your 'A' and 'B' goals.

Keeping *focused*

Finally, you need to stay focused on these goals. At the start of the season or training phase all athletes have the best intentions. Goals are set, races are entered and the training feels good. But as the meat of the season kicks in, it is all too easy to forget about the original goals, or

below Goals need to be challenging, realistic and specific.

above Mirinda Carfrae targeted her cycling times for improvement.

adjust targets that may seem too challenging. When this happens, the likelihood is that the original goals will slip away. To prevent this you can do two very simple things:

WRITE THE GOALS DOWN AND STICK THEM SOMEWHERE VISIBLE

This might sound simplistic, but if you have a paper copy of your goals stuck in a place that you see every day or every few days, then you will always be reminded about your original targets. It doesn't matter where this place is (stuck to the front of the fridge, put at the front of a training diary, pinned to the side of a desk, etc.), this piece of paper just needs to be visible.

READ THE GOALS

Once you have written these goals down, you need to read them regularly. The piece of paper should ideally be in a place where you have to read it, but if it is not you need to make a mental note to read these goals on a regular basis (perhaps once per week) and remind yourself of what you are working towards. Keeping these goals in the forefront of your mind will help you to stay focused on them.

Goals are essential. What's more, every athlete who commits to an endurance event has them (even if that goal is simply to finish). Establishing a series of specific, challenging goals is therefore a key part of the endurance athlete's training phase. These goals will ultimately be the motivation that drives every endurance athlete towards the finishing line.

Overhauling a
performance
MIRINDA CARFRAE

The 2012 Ironman World Championships was Mirinda Carfrae's fourth race on Hawaii's Big Island. In 2009 – her first attempt at the event commonly referred to as Kona – she finished second to Chrissie Wellington; in 2010 she won the race outright; and in 2011 she once again finished second to Wellington. In each of those three races she shattered her own course run record. In 2012 Carfrae set the ambitious goal of overhauling her race strategy so that it was not so run focused. She was, in part, motivated to do that after her experience at the previous Ironman World Championships.

The women's race at the 2011 Ironman World Championships is widely remembered for being the race in which Chrissie Wellington overcame adversity to claim her fourth Kona title. Wellington was involved in a serious bike crash just weeks before the race, and open scars were evident as she battled her way to a historic victory. Carfrae pushed her hard. In fact, the Australian came within two minutes of the Briton on the marathon before ultimately finishing just under three minutes back (Wellington finished in 8 hours, 55 minutes and 8 seconds, Carfrae in 8 hours, 57 minutes and 57 seconds). Carfrae swam faster than Wellington (Carfrae exited the water in 57 minutes and 17 seconds to Wellington's 1 hour, 1 minute and 3 seconds) and ran faster than the Brit (2 hours, 52 minutes and 9 seconds against 2 hours, 52 minutes and 41 seconds), but she lost a lot of time on the bike. In fact, Wellington's 4 hours, 56 minutes and 53 seconds was more than seven minutes faster than Carfrae's 5 hours, 4 minutes and 17 seconds. It was a significant difference and it cost Carfrae the title.

In light of her defeat, the Australian re-evaluated her goals for the 2012 season:

> **I sat down** at the end of the year and looked at my results in the past and looked at where women's triathlon and Ironman was going and it's pretty evident

that women were starting to cycle very fast. And for me to continue to race well and be competitive I felt that I really needed to improve my cycling. And that meant changing my programme focus. Obviously you can't really take your eye off the ball in any of the three disciplines but I had been quite run focused – I was able to run well and do well.

> But the sport is evolving and the times are coming down and if I want to continue to compete at that level I needed to improve my cycling ability and still keep my run around the same level.

Carfrae's reaction was partly driven by perception, and partly by her desire to be a better athlete:

> **After Kona** [2011] I just got sick of being called a runner. You want to be an all-round athlete. I perceived, and it was evident, that the cycle was letting me down a little bit. So when I sat down and looked at things it was pretty clear that I could make up the most amount of time on the bike. You can always improve on swimming, but it's only a matter of minutes. But with the bike leg there's a lot of time to be made so that's where we focused most of our attention.

> From there I left my coach of seven years at the beginning of the year – not for any other reason than I felt it was time to seek out other opinions and try a different approach. So I started working with a guy called Mat Steinmetz a little bit. He was advising me on my cycling and how to structure my programme with a little more cycle focus so I could improve it.

Having identified a key performance goal for the 2012 season, Carfrae set about establishing targets to help her realise that goal. Like the majority of long-distance triathletes, Carfrae identified the Ironman World Championships as the place where she would benchmark her development.

> **That race demands** your 100 per cent attention. The reason I've been successful the last three years is because it's the race I build up to all year and it's

the race I think about when I'm training hard. It's the big one.

To measure her progress towards her goals, Carfrae structured her preparation around races that would see her peak at the Ironman World Championships. However, by her own admission, her competitive performances going into Hawaii were inconsistent (largely due to illness), affecting her confidence.

❝ *You never really know* what's going to happen. Obviously you're trying to improve all the time. But completely changing the way you approach training when that plan was very successful was always going to be a bit of a risk. I had to see whether it would pay off or not. I was definitely a bit nervous about making the changes but I believed that in the long run it will be the best thing for me. In the short term it takes a little while – sometimes you have to take a couple of steps back before you start reaping the rewards.

If her race season hadn't quite panned out as anticipated, the training had. After overhauling her bike position and adopting the use of technology available to her, the Australian began to see the results.

❝ *I had key sessions* in training. I started to use a power meter in training and the numbers are black and white – they don't lie. We had goals throughout the year and I was definitely seeing the improvement in training

below Carfrae made a name for herself chasing down her opponents on the run.

What's more, despite predominantly focusing on building her bike strength, Carfrae was still managing to hit her run numbers in training.

> ❝ **In training** my running has been pretty much around the level that it has been in past years and certainly in the couple of races I've done the run has been in the same ballpark. But I feel that in the last couple of races I've done it's felt harder to produce similar times. I think I'm working harder on the bike so that's taking more energy out of me for the run so it's a bit of an adapting period. Especially in terms of nutrition. In the middle of the year I rode really well but I ran out of calories. So what I would normally take on the bike wasn't enough for working at a higher level so I've had to make adjustments in nutrition as well.

Going into the 2012 Ironman World Championships Mirinda Carfrae was undoubtedly one of the favourites for the title. However, on a hot, windy day in Hawaii, she was unable to secure her second crown. Emerging from the water in 1 hour and 6 seconds, Carfrae was just under three minutes down on her 2011 time – although tough conditions affected the times of every athlete. Her bike, too, was slower (5 hours, 12 minutes and 18 seconds in 2012 compared to 5 hours, 4 minutes and 17 seconds in 2011). Despite the slower split time, though, Carfrae began the run closer to the leaders than ever before (just 8 minutes and 9 seconds back from Caroline Steffen who was first on to the run). However, this time she did not have the legs to take the win. A 3 hours, 5 minutes and 4 seconds marathon – more than 13 minutes slower than her 2011 race – saw her finish third overall.

A number of factors affected Carfrae's performance on the day. As mentioned, extreme heat and high winds made for slow racing and impacted the finish times of every athlete. Carfrae also lost a feed bottle in the latter stages of the bike, which she believes had a negative impact on her run performance.

As such, her failure to win her second Kona title in 2012 cannot simply be put down to her change in training goals. If anything, the fact that she was able to finish the bike leg of the race closer to the leaders than ever before is testimony to the fact that a lot of her work during the year had in fact paid off – something that Carfrae herself contends:

> ❝ **I feel like** my preparation in 2012 was pretty good. I was in fantastic shape and looking back on the race I think I was ready to contend for the title. It was just a matter of making mistakes within the race – maybe dropping the ball on nutrition a little bit and not staying on top of things throughout the bike race, and that really cost me in the back half of the marathon.

below Carfrae struggled at the 2012 Ironman World Championships.

Needless to say, this work continued to pay dividends going into the 2013 season. Following the race in 2012 Carfrae made some important changes. She returned to her former coach, Siri Lindley, and re-evaluated her targets accordingly:

> *We [Carfrae and Lindley]* didn't sit down and go over goals for the race as I've had a similar set of goals since I started racing Kona. So she said: 'I'm not going to go through what your goals are as I know what they are – to win Kona'. So we were on the same page.

From that point onwards it was a question of learning from the race in 2012 and keeping her performance moving forward:

> *Going into 2013* I was in really good shape and ready to race for the world title. After learning the lessons of 2012 the hard way in terms of nutrition I definitely had a Plan B and a Plan C if I lost the water bottle like I did in 2012.

The preparation and the training paid off. Carfrae not only secured her second Ironman World Championship, but she also broke the Kona course record (8 hours, 52 minutes, and 14 seconds). Along the way she shattered the run course record (2 hours, 50 minutes and 38 seconds) and became the first female champion to run a faster marathon than the male winner at Kona. It was an outstanding performance in what Carfrae describes as a perfect race.

> *We had really* good conditions and that helped to bring the times down nicely. It was a perfect storm – I felt great.

Mirinda Carfrae's differing experiences in 2012 and 2013 demonstrate two things:

1. Athletes need a strategy that can adapt to changing variables in a race (for more on this see Chapter 10: Adaptation).

2. Some goals take longer to realise than others – particularly when it comes to specific aspects of performance.

Carfrae's work throughout 2012 undoubtedly set her up for a simply outstanding victory in 2013. Her title-winning bike split of 4 hours, 58 minutes and 20 seconds was just three minutes slower than that of the fastest female pro on the day, Meredith Kessler (4 hours, 55 minutes and 13 seconds). What's more, while Kessler traded the lead with two other cyclists, Carfrae rode most of the 180km bike solo. That feat alone demonstrates that the work she did throughout 2012 (and of course in preparation for 2013) had paid off.

Every athlete needs goals. It is what drives individuals to train and to perform. Occasionally those goals can impact short-term confidence. However, if the athlete can establish specific goals and back those up with an effective training phase, then they should realise improvements in their race-day performance. How the athlete builds out their training phase is, however, just as important as how they establish their goals, and that is what we discuss in the next chapter.

GOAL SETTING: KEY POINTS

- Goal setting falls into three groups: 'A', 'B' and immediate goals.
- 'A' goals need to be realistic, challenging and specific.
- 'B' goals need to be specific to particular events and training phases.
- Immediate goals are technique or target orientated.
- Goals need to be clearly established and placed somewhere obvious where you will read them every day.
- Do not be afraid to set targets that challenge aspects of your performance.

Training:
Building confidence through preparation

There are many factors involved in successfully preparing the mind for competition. However, few are as important as the confidence gained from a well-executed training plan. If an athlete follows a plan that they believe prepares them properly for race day, then they will go into an event with a heightened state of confidence, and are thus more likely to realise their goals.

Managing training volumes for endurance events is not easy. Professional athletes dedicate their lives to it, while more often than not amateur athletes struggle to juggle the high volume sessions with their work, family and social life (more on that in Chapter 5 – The team: Finding the right balance).

However, with careful planning and the right approach, this does not have to be the case. Of course, few amateurs are going to be able to match the quite staggering training volumes executed by the world's leading endurance athletes. During peak training phases ultra-runner Dean Karnazes famously attempts to complete a marathon before breakfast. Olympic Silver medallist and ten-times marathon swimming world champion Thomas Lurz can swim anywhere up to 110 kilometres in a week. Meanwhile, multiple Ironman World Champion Craig Alexander indulges in a three- to five-week 'peak phase' leading into the 'A' race for the season. During this phase Alexander will typically train between 40 and 45 hours per week, swimming 20–25km, cycling 650–700km, and running around 120km. He will also make multiple visits to the gym and significant recovery periods are built into that schedule, including massages, ice baths and compression booths. Alexander understandably views it as 'a full-time job'.

The majority of the athletes interviewed for this book are either professionals or individuals who have been able to build their lives around their chosen sport. This is not a luxury enjoyed by most amateur athletes, and as such one of the primary goals for every non-professional should be to develop an effective, realistic training regimen that complements all aspects of their lives. As arguably the world's most successful triathlon coach, Brett Sutton, says:

> ❝ **The only difference** between a pro and an age grouper is that a pro has more time and they are faster.

Rachael **CADMAN**

❝ I worked out where the key sessions were, looked at what I was building up to and how to get there without having to swim six times a week. I applied that to all three sports and that's how I put together a bit of a programme

Factoring significant training volumes into their lives does not mean that the athlete should abandon their goals. Of course, if an amateur athlete seriously expects to compete with a professional, they not only have to possess exceptional natural abilities, but will also need to put in significant, highly targeted training volumes to do so (and have to consider the feasibility of doing that). But if that same athlete is content with being competitive in the amateur ranks, then it is possible to develop a training schedule that allows this while maintaining a good balance with other areas of their life: work, family and friends.

To do so, though, the amateur athlete needs to start thinking like a pro. That begins with identifying the areas of their performance that require the most development, and targeting those areas during quality training sessions. Quality is the operative word in training under these circumstances. The temptation with endurance sports is to build a significant base with scant attention to the high-end work that separates the good from the exceptional. Of course, base is important. But just as professional athletes target base, build and peak phases, so should every amateur endurance athlete.

The intricacies of training phases is beyond the remit of this book. However, adopting a professional approach to preparing for an event is not. Of course, every event is different – as is every athlete. But by adopting a targeted, professional approach to training, you will arrive at the starting line not only physically prepared, but confident that you can succeed in meeting your goals. That confidence is an invaluable weapon on race day.

Adopting a professional approach to *preparation*
RACHAEL CADMAN

Developing a highly targeted, professional approach to training is exactly what Rachael Cadman did when she decided to attempt the Enduroman Arch to Arc. Cadman was bidding to become the first woman (and only the eighth person in the history of the race) to complete one of the world's longest, toughest triathlons. Combining three ultra-distance disciplines, the Arch to Arc begins with an 87-mile run from Marble Arch in the centre of London to Dover Harbour on England's south coast. After (usually) overnighting in Dover the athlete then swims across the English Channel (the distance ranges from 21–35 miles depending on the tide), before completing a 181-mile cycle ride to the Arc de Triomphe in Paris. According to the rules of the race, athletes have 13 days in which to complete the

event, but most finish in around four (rests and overnight stops included). Mark Bayliss is the current world record holder for the Arch to Arc, finishing in 73 hours, 39 minutes and 12 seconds. To register that time Bayliss completed the run in 26 hours and 20 minutes; the swim in 11 hours and 48 minutes (Bayliss chose not to use a wetsuit for the swim – he was the first competitor not to do so) and the bike in 18 hours and 9 minutes – with around 17 hours of rest/waiting time.

It is worth noting that the waiting time factored into this event is largely dominated by the tides in the English Channel. Boasting one of the most aggressive tidal systems in the world, athletes have very small windows of opportunity to swim the Channel, and as such the organisers will make them wait in Dover until the swim conditions are deemed both suitable and safe to attempt a crossing.

The Enduroman Arch to Arc is a formidable challenge. Independently, the three legs of the race (and in particular the run and the swim) are enough to test the mettle of the strongest athletes in those particular disciplines. Combined, it is a truly epic physical and mental challenge.

Of course, the sheer distance of the event – let alone the back-to-back execution of the different disciplines – means that the Arch to Arc is not an easy race to prepare for. However, Cadman's preparation was even more challenging because she was juggling significant training volumes with a full-time job. She also chose not to employ the services of a coach for the 24-month training period. Of course, she did plenty of research and spoke to people who could help her. But ultimately she set her own targets, determined her own sessions and took responsibility for managing her body through the process.

From the outset, Cadman prioritised the parts of the race that she felt needed the most attention. In particular, she focused on those areas that she felt represented significant barriers to completing the race.

left 'I think you have to pick your battles' – Rachael Cadman

❝ **I always felt** that if the swim was okay I could do the run and cycle. So my big focus was to get into good enough shape to be able to do the swim. It wasn't difficult to leave the cycling alone because I just couldn't find that time to train. If I had tried to cram any more big stuff in I think it would have been detrimental – I think you have to pick your battles. For me the swim was the battle so I focused on that and hoped that everything else would come together.

Of course, this focus on the swim did not mean that she neglected other areas of her training. Rather, it provided the focal point of her training around which the plan could be built. By constructing her training plan in this way, she was able to build confidence in her preparation, even if it did waver from time to time.

❝ **The Channel** swimming guys were swimming six times a week which obviously wasn't going to work when I had the volume of training that I had to do. So I worked out where the key sessions were, looked at what I was building up to and how to get there without having to swim six times a week. I applied that to all three sports and that's how I put together a bit of a programme. I did have moments where I thought it could have all gone to pot, but I think with ultra-distance events most people are pretty self-aware and are quite comfortable with how much they can suffer in themselves. I tend to think that the best person who knows that is me, so I was confident enough to build my own programme around what I felt I could do.

Cadman's confidence was built on the work that she had done to formulate this plan. Like any good student of their sport she did plenty of research, read as many articles as she could and spoke to a lot of people. Throughout this process she was also careful to be selective of the information that she chose to take on board, and that which she chose to discard.

❝ **Lots of people** were saying 'you've got to do all this hard training' and 'train hard, race easy' but

above Training for a race of such massive distances is a puzzle in itself.

above Cadman's main focus was to be in shape enough to handle the Channel swim.

that's ridiculous when you're thinking about the kind of event you're going to do. And I thought 'those kind of things are not going to work for me, I need to be kinder to myself as I'm working full-time, I've got a fiancé and things I need to do.' For me, I needed to pick key points of focus and work around those rather than absorb everything.

Identifying individuals whose advice you can trust is essential for any athlete, regardless of the level at which they train and race (see Chapter 5 – The team: Finding the right balance). All amateur athletes can benefit from filtering the information that is shared with them, and carefully determining which bits apply to them and which can be discarded. Once useful information has been identified, it needs to be moulded and adapted to fit in with the individual's circumstances. Only the athlete knows how much time and effort they can and should be putting into their sport. As such, only the athlete can decide which advice is useful and which isn't.

Cadman's journey to London's Marble Arch was long and at times tortuous. The Brit prepared over two years for the event, and along the way it was natural that there were doubts and concerns.

❝ I guess there is always the concern that you are doing it all totally wrong and that you don't know what you're doing. And I had these moments thinking 'God, I've trained myself and I might have got it totally wrong and all these people are relying on me and maybe I'm not capable of it.'

It's really difficult because I had milestones in terms of things I had done with endurance – if you're doing an Ironman you can see your times getting better or if you do a tempo session it might feel better. I didn't really have that level of progression – I didn't feel really strong or fit. All my sessions I would just get in and do them – nothing was really time-orientated. So I did have moments where I wondered if I had done the wrong stuff.

The Arch to Arc is a relatively unique event. As Cadman says, in every sport there are performance benchmarks (set distance split times, average speeds, etc.) against which the athlete can rate him or herself. Training progression against these benchmarks can be analysed throughout the preparatory phase and so the athlete can build confidence by measuring improvements in their performance. The distances involved in the Arch to Arc, however, make such benchmarks almost impossible to identify. In addition, it was difficult for Cadman to work out how she was going to perform on race day because she was going to expose her body to such a prolonged period of sustained exercise.

To help grow her confidence in that area Cadman established a series of 'B' goals in build-up races to train her body to cope with sustained exposure to high-intensity exercise. These races were also invaluable for learning what she could and could not tolerate under stressful

circumstances. Cadman completed Ironman Switzerland (3.9km swim, 180km bike, 42.2km run in 12 hours, 43 minutes and 52 seconds) just two weeks before racing the Double Ironman (7.2km swim, 360km bike, 84.4km run).

I said to myself that I would go steady in Switzerland and use it as a really good training day, and then have two weeks' taper and then do the Double Ironman. I basically did marathon training all the way up to the Double Ironman – I don't think I ran more than 26 miles – which was a bit of a strange strategy. But I thought I would just have to see how I went on the day as I couldn't fit anything else in.

The plan for the Double Ironman was to see what kind of things I liked to eat when I am fatigued, how running and cycling at night works, how long runs worked, what equipment I'd need. There was nothing really for the swim because the swim was so different to the Arch to Arc swim that I didn't think I could take anything from that, but there were lots that I thought I could cross-transfer from the run and the cycle. Those

below With preparation comes the knowledge that you can be successful on race day.

were the aims. There wasn't any sort of time aim, it was all about what can I get from this? I still wanted to do well, obviously, because it's an event and I'm an athlete, but I had nothing specific. The only goal I set for that was that I wanted to be the first woman out of the swim and do it in under 2 hours and 20 minutes, which was the target. That was the only thing I could control and knew about. I had never done 224 miles on the bike or a double marathon, but I knew about the swim.

Cadman's approach to the Double Ironman (itself a supreme test of physical fitness) was typical of the strategies employed by professional athletes across the

above Properly executed training plans build confidence.

sporting spectrum. She had a very clearly defined 'A' race that she was building towards during the course of her training period, but was using 'B' races to monitor her progress during that build-up period and learn what she needed to do when it came to executing during the event (in terms of fuel, hydration and management of fatigue). By adopting this strategy, Cadman was able to build up her confidence about what she could achieve on the training volumes she had set herself, and so refine her training plan to work on the areas that she felt needed most attention.

❝ *I was self-coached* and not many people had done the Arch to Arc so I could have got swept up in feeling that I had to do loads of stuff. The great thing about the Double Ironman was that I had only run 26 miles in training and managed to run 52; I'd only cycled 160 miles and managed to do 224. Taking that away was one of the biggest things I learnt because it meant that I could go and do a 50-mile run and I knew it would get me through 80 miles. Knowing that I didn't have to do that in training was really helpful.

This is perhaps the one area where Cadman differed significantly from the pros in the ways that she prepared. Many professional athletes will train beyond the distances required for their event. Indeed, some will even train beyond those distances at above race pace, to boost their confidence ahead of the event. Torbjørn Sindballe was an Ironman triathlete famous for his strength on the bike. To prepare for the Ironman World Championships Sindballe used to ride for seven hours at race pace in Kona, Hawaii to make the actual race 'feel like a training ride'. Craig Alexander, meanwhile, will sometimes run the last half an hour of a two-and-a-half hour training run above race pace. These sessions instil the confidence and belief required to perform on the day.

However, for amateur athletes who struggle to manage their time, taking the opposite approach can also work. If the goal is to complete in a reasonable time, the athlete does not have to complete race distances in their build-up. There is no denying that it is a significant advantage to do so. Nor is this a pass out from tough sessions – they have to be completed (Cadman completed 10-hour swim sessions and 50-mile runs during her preparation). But if time is tight and the goals are more modest than, say, a world record, then it is amazing how much can be achieved on lesser volumes.

What's more, if the training is done properly and is backed up by good preparatory races, the athlete will have the confidence to perform. This is how Cadman felt on race day:

> ❝ *I felt confident.* I did have moments where I wondered if I had done the wrong stuff. It was difficult at the time as I didn't want to jinx anything but I felt really confident that I was going to do it. That was partly my support team as well. They instilled a confidence in me that it would be fine. But I didn't want to say 'oh, it will be fine' and then be the person for who wasn't fine and feel stupid.

Cadman's approach to completing the Arch to Arc was as professional as it was pragmatic. She successfully finished the race on 19 August 2011, running the 87 miles from London to Dover in 23 hours, 21 minutes and 8 seconds. After a 24-hour stopover in Dover, Cadman swam the Channel in 16 hours and 33 minutes, despite the best efforts of a turning tide to derail her bid. After a 13-hour pause in Calais, Cadman battled torrential rain and fatigue en route to the Champs-Élysées where she completed the Arch to Arc cycle in 20 hours and 16 minutes. Her overall time (97 hours and 37 minutes) was the fourth fastest in the history of the race at that time, and she was the only woman to have completed the event.

It would have been very easy for Rachael Cadman to get carried away with the enormity of the task that faced her when she set off from Marble Arch. But it would have been even easier for Cadman to have been put off by the volume of training – not to mention the length of time that she was building up to the event – that she had to do before she even approached the starting line.

However, by adopting a highly targeted, well-executed approach to a training regimen that placed significant demands on her time, Cadman developed the confidence to successfully realise the ambitious goals that she had set herself.

A coach's *perspective*
BRETT SUTTON

Anyone can coach. Not everyone can coach well. As endurance sports flourish the number of coaches has grown accordingly. So have the various styles of coaching. From one-on-one weekly (or more) sessions to virtual coaching via the Internet, athletes are exposing themselves to more and more advice – good and bad – from coaches who profess to know the ins and outs of a sport. That's not to say that they don't. There are many exceptionally talented swim, run, triathlon, bike and pretty-much-any-endurance-sport-you-can-think-of coaches around the world. What's more, they can have a profound and positive impact on an athlete's performance. But for a coach to really be able to shape the development of an athlete and instil in them the confidence to perform, they have to do more than simply prescribe training sessions. They need to know the athlete, appreciate the differences in the physiological and psychological make-up of their 'team', and adjust their training strategies according to each athlete's needs and wants.

One man who is arguably the greatest exponent of this strategy of coaching in triathlon is Brett Sutton. A former Australian boxing champion with a background coaching everything from greyhounds to Ironman triathletes, Sutton's approach is relatively simple: he views every athlete as psychologically and physiologically unique, looks at what makes them tick and builds a training plan around them accordingly. History indicates that this strategy works. Sutton has coached numerous world and Olympic champions. What's more, as the former head coach at teamTBB Sutton can also claim to have coached more Ironman champions than any other coach currently operating in the sport. Alongside London 2012 Olympic Gold Medallist Nicola Spirig (more on her in Chapter 14 – When it all comes together) Sutton's most famous squad member was Chrissie Wellington. Undefeated over Ironman distance, Sutton helped to nurture Wellington from being 2006 amateur short-course age group world champion to 2007 Ironman world champion – a startling progression for any athlete and in such a short period of time.

But while Wellington and Sutton made the transition from good amateur to leading professional look relatively easy, managing Wellington's development as a long-course triathlete was not, at least at the beginning of the process.

❝ **Chrissie was** physically precocious when she turned up and I thought that if I could get a handle on her I could make her a great athlete.

The main battle that Sutton faced was harnessing Wellington's desire to work hard. That may sound counter-intuitive, but the key for any endurance athlete is to tread the fine line between working hard and working too hard. When the athlete works hard they grow in confidence and ability. When they work too hard, burn-out is usually not too far behind. Sutton was conscious that that was a risk with an athlete of Wellington's mentality.

❝ **I didn't let her** go flat out at anything when I was coaching her because she's a lunatic. It didn't matter whether she was washing the dishes or running – whether it was 4km or 40km – it was always the same: flat out. I realised that and harnessed it.

But the fact of the matter was that when she left, people said 'She's going to be winning for the next ten years.' I said 'She won't be in the sport in two years' because of the people she was training with. You

right Most athletes have to make their training programmes work around their lives.

know, they would say: 'Look at that session, I reckon you can get two seconds faster.' We never did that. She'd be the first to tell you that when she pushed too hard I used to stop her training, that's how I used to discipline her. When she was tired and I knew she was tired – but she wouldn't say she was tired – I'd give her two days' suspension: she wasn't allowed out of her room to train.

If she had had that over the last three years then she'd be in the sport for another ten because nobody can get near her – she's that good. She's a phenomenal athlete. But they burnt her out – every session for her is a burn out. She'll go until she drops three times a day which is fine because physically she's built like a horse – she's as strong as you can go – but you know what burns? The thing between your ears.

Wellington parted ways with Sutton in 2008 after two successful years, which saw her claim five Ironman victories – including two world championships – and numerous wins at other international events. Under a new coach she went on to win another eight Ironman races – including two more world championships – over three years, before surprising everyone at the end of 2011 and announcing that she wanted to take some time away from the sport. 'She just burnt herself to a frazzle,' Sutton says.

❝ **All of this** back-slapping and 'you did 8:30'. I had her doing races where when she won she had basically been walking.

A good coach realises what he has on his hands: she was a real person that you couldn't give full rein too. If you do that she'll kill herself.

Sutton's approach to coaching Wellington is no different from his approach to coaching all of his athletes. He looks at the individual and determines what they need to work on physically and mentally to realise their goals.

above Chrissie Wellington claims yet another Ironman World Championship victory.

' **My job is** to not over-coach. Ninety per cent of the problems with most coaches is that they over-coach and wreck kids because they are trying too hard to prove themselves. Back in the day – and this is one of the smartest things I've ever heard – a guy told me: 'you know the difference between a great coach and a good one? The great one knows what to say and knows when not to say it.'

People will tell you that I'm very minimalistic and don't say much, but when I do tell them something it resonates. I'll disagree with something technical – a stroke or something – and then I'll weigh up the other options plus the mentality of the person. I ask myself, what's it going to do if I change it? Of course, theoretically I'm going to make them a better swimmer.

But is it going to make them a better swimmer psychologically? Are they going to think 'There's something wrong with my swim stroke, I've got to fix it?' You try for a 2 per cent improvement and all of a sudden you get a 5 per cent deficit because of three or four other psychological values. Those are the things that I'm trying to teach my coaches, and they are that things that are more important than what you read in books. I'll look at one person and say 'Yes, I'll change her stroke because she'll cope with it and it'll make her better and she won't have a drama.' But I might say 'If I start tinkering with this guy he's going to go slower.'

You've heard it 100 times before when a guy wins races and people say 'But his stroke is shit. If he just altered his stroke he would swim faster.' Well, it's not that easy. A lot of coaches don't get it. They go in with their 1–2–3 and they destroy athletes by trying to teach them to be theoretically better.

I don't have that problem because I'm used to dealing with animals. You can't sit there and talk to a horse. If you've got a frightened horse you've got to know your horse and you've got to know when to say 'I can't do that with him because if I do it it's going to fall to pieces.' That's basically how I look at my athletes. It's the same thing, I psychologically profile them and then I train them to how I think their profile is. It's the same as I physically profile them.

Sutton breeds confidence in his athletes by making them challenge their own limits. His athletes are given target numbers at the start of a training phase, and the training sessions that he sets them build towards those numbers. This approach to training is explored further in Chapter 14 – When it all comes together. Results dictate that this confidence transfers into performance.

❝ **We really hammer home** the fact that if these are your set of numbers, this is what you should be aiming at and you should be fit enough so that when you get to 5 kilometres to go, if you have to stretch it then we stretch it. Up until that point everyone in my group is educated to stick to what they are capable of and they know that because that is what they do in training.

In Ironman you've got to stick to your numbers. It's no good saying you're going to smash it. You're not going to smash anything apart from yourself.

A good coach recognises that not all of his team are built equal. The best coaches develop training and race strategies around these differences. Sutton has enjoyed unprecedented levels of success because of this approach to training and racing. Of course, not every athlete can – or would choose to – work with a coach. Even so, the ideology that Sutton expounds when it comes to coaching rings true for the self-taught athlete.

Every athlete is an individual and every individual has to balance different priorities and realise different goals. The key for every individual is to find the balance between hard training and an acceptable lifestyle. The athlete – and the coach – that is able to do that will undoubtedly realise the improved performances that they so often seek.

A word on training
motivation

Training for endurance sports is notoriously tough. In fact, many athletes will tell you that it is harder than completing the event itself. Athletes subject their bodies and minds to months – and, in some cases, years – of hard work attempting to realise a specific goal. And while managing the body through this process is unquestionably difficult, the process of managing the mind is arguably harder. After all, it is the mind that drives the body along the road to success.

Training for endurance events must begin (and to an extent, end) with the realisation that every athlete is an individual. As such, predefined training programmes – the one-size-fits-all model – of athletic development are limited in their uses. That is not to say that they are useless – that is far from the truth. Rather, they should be used as a guide rather than a finished strategy for realising an athlete's goals. Instead, athletes need to begin their preparation by making an honest appraisal of their own abilities – both good and bad. From that point forward, they can start to develop a long-term strategy that will help them to develop specific aspects of their performance.

Crucially, though, this strategy has to be realistic. It is almost impossible for an athlete who works a 60-hour week to fit in 20 hours of training if they intend to have a family or social life. Of course, it can be done. But an athlete who chooses to do that must also realise that there is a very significant risk of neglecting areas of their life or burning out one or two years down the road. As a result, every endurance athlete should sit down at the planning stage of their training and build their strategy around the demands of both their life and performance. Taking these considerations into account will place less stress on the athlete, and as Brett Sutton says: 'a happy athlete is a fast athlete'.

Finding this balance is what we deal with in the next chapter.

TRAINING: KEY POINTS

- Training plans need to focused and realistic: if you cannot fit in 20 hours of training per week then do not write a 20 hour per week schedule!
- Identify the areas of performance that are the greatest barriers to realising your goals.
- In endurance sports it is amazing that so much can sometimes be achieved on so little. Quality not quantity!
- Predetermined training plans do not suit everybody. All athletes are different and training plans need to be adapted to suit the needs and psychology of the individual.
- Do your homework. Talk to people and read relevant articles before drawing up a comprehensive training plan.

5

The team:
Finding the right balance

Stability. Every human being craves it – or at least aspects of it – and the more you speak or listen to athletes, the more you will hear them referencing how important it is. The best athletes in the world – from runners to tennis players to footballers – frequently cite the importance of having a stable unit around them to be able to perform at their best. Endurance athletes are no different. In fact, because of the nature of endurance sports and the demands that these pursuits place on the body, mind and time of endurance athletes, a stable team environment is a key facet to success.

At this stage, it is important to define what we mean by team. In sporting terms, an athlete's team is made up of the people (or even the person) who directly help them to realise their goals. In this regard, a professional athlete's team might consist of a coach, a physiotherapist and/or an agent (some athletes have extended teams with all sorts of peripheral figures). Endurance sports are slightly different.

Of course, some endurance athletes have a 'conventional' sporting team around them. But because the financial rewards in endurance sports are significantly smaller than those in mainstream sports, typically an athlete who participates in these events does not enjoy the attentions of a dedicated team. In fact, as we have already seen, numerous professional athletes manage their own coaching schedules and travel to races alone. And when they are not alone, more often than not they are supported by their families and/or friends.

In these cases, family and friends become the team. What's more, they will almost always be the most passionate members of the team. With that in mind, many full-time (or near full-time) athletes work hard to develop a regimen that allows them to balance their sporting and personal lives. As ultra-marathon runner Dean Karnazes puts it:

❝ **I get up** at four in the morning and run. When I'm really training hard I try to run a marathon before breakfast. Then I fix breakfast and get my kids off to school every day and then while they are in school I'll do a shorter tempo run in the afternoon – you know, speed work. And then I round them up from school and we all have dinner together.

It's more quality than quantity. When I am around and I am not competing then I'm all theirs: I'm not distracted. I turn off my phone when I'm home –

I'm all there. They are so sick of me when I'm around that they are like 'Dad, when are you leaving again?'

Three-time Ironman World Champion Craig Alexander has a similar perspective.

> ❝ **Essentially all I have** to do each day – and we keep it very simple and I like that – is be dad and train. I've been able to do that – find a nice balance so that I don't feel guilty about leaving the kids – because I certainly don't want them to think that what I'm doing is more important to me than them. But essentially, it's still my job and I'm lucky I've got a very supportive wife, and with time management she makes sure I don't miss out on anything. That makes me happy and

above A stable unit of people around us help us to perform at our best.

I think that when you're in an emotionally good place your training is much better. I've been lucky to have that steadying influence from my wife.

Of course, both Karnazes and Alexander enjoy slightly different realities to the majority of endurance athletes. Karnazes has developed a successful media career that dovetails with his running, while Alexander is a full-time professional Ironman triathlete. However, both have adopted training regimens that allow them to find balance in their lives.

Finding that balance is difficult for many amateur endurance athletes. Because of the nature of the pursuit, a serious endurance athlete can spend anything up to 30 hours per week training. If that athlete is not a professional, that means juggling work (an additional 40-plus hours per week), family/friend time, training and, at some point, rest. In short, endurance sports represent a significant time investment for many athletes and external commitments can be tough to balance

However, finding that balance is essential. Not least because it will have a direct impact on an athlete's performance. Not only will an athlete benefit from the support of family and friends, but the positivity that comes from a balanced approach will be carried into performance. It's simple: if family and friends are happy and encourage the athlete's endeavours, then their mental state will be enhanced. Legendary triathlon coach Brett Sutton agrees:

> ❝ **The only difference** between a pro and an age group athlete is that they have more time and they are faster. If you're an age grouper and you have a family of three kids and a high-profile job, then trying to push faster and harder is selfish. You have to use the sport for enjoyment and make it fit in with your job or your family. You can benefit from the health benefits. I see so many people cooking themselves because they want to go 10 minutes quicker but struggle because they have to do things like go away for business. They have to factor it all in because I factor it in with my guys.

I have a couple in my squad – they're pros – and if I see them have a fight I won't send them out for the session they had in the afternoon if it's a hard session, I'll send them for an easy run. Because the psychological profile doesn't change if you are a little slower. If you are stressed mentally and then go out and stress yourself physically you're only going to make the mental stress worse.

It comes down to the simplest thing: a happy athlete is a fast athlete.

Finding an effective balance between home and sporting life will lead to rewards in training and racing. It is that simple. But it is not easy to do and, like so many things, it takes constant work. However, the fact of the matter is that if you have a supportive, stable unit around you, you will ultimately carry the positivity of that unit into your performance, and your performance will benefit as a result. As such, it is most definitely an effort worth making.

Dipping into the talent *pool*

As a general rule, endurance athletes are a competitive bunch. As such, when athletes train as part of a group there are always individuals looking to push the pace, break the 'competition' (otherwise known as training partners) and claim a Saturday morning 'win'. That level of friendly competition is not only healthy, but helps to maintain motivation.

However, it can also be an invaluable tool in determining the areas of performance that need the most work. Training partners invariably, and often silently, analyse the strengths and weaknesses of the people that they run, swim or ride with. These weaknesses are frequently the areas that they will exploit during training sessions, and would certainly do so in a competitive race scenario. In short, these are the areas that an athlete needs to work on if they are to find the improvements in performance that they are chasing during each and every session.

above Having the support of family and friends is essential to being successful.

In lieu of a coach (if you have one, all the better), it makes perfect sense to consider making training partners part of the 'team'. Of course, you need to be careful to choose individuals that you not only trust, but also respect. But once you have selected those individuals, they should be invited to provide honest and constructive assessments of your strengths and weaknesses. In so doing, they will help you construct a training plan that will start to address the weaknesses in your performance.

Needless to say, you might not agree with the assessments of your training partners when it comes to determining those weaknesses. If that is the case, then you alone must decide what you feel comfortable working on during the training phase of your preparation. Regardless of whether you agree with your training partners or not, inviting the feedback of those whom you know best will undoubtedly lead to assessments and suggestions that can shape and hone your physical development.

This is something that even the best in the world do. Admittedly, when three-time Ironman World Champion Craig Alexander seeks the guidance of those around him, he is not necessarily talking to the training buddies that he regularly swims, cycles or runs with. However, he most definitely seeks the advice and thoughts of carefully selected individuals whose judgement he trusts and whom undoubtedly follow his progress throughout the course of a season.

> ❝ *I seek the advice* of people I respect, and I cross-match their suggestions with what I've come up with and in an uncanny fashion it's always very similar.
>
> I talk to the people who know me best and who have known me as an athlete for a long time and the people whose opinion I respect because of their knowledge and experience – they are the people whose advice I seek out. There are usually two or three of them and the suggestions that they make are usually pretty close to what I've come up with myself. I think that's the first part of the puzzle.

Like Alexander, once those ideas have been gathered together you must then decide how to turn ideas into execution. In most cases, athletes will draw up a training plan and follow that plan through to its conclusion. However, once again this training plan is something that can be shared with the 'team'. Sharing ideas with other athletes merely gives you a greater pool of knowledge and expertise to dip into. In so doing there is the potential to uncover training techniques and sessions that have been hitherto overlooked and which could lead

to significant improvements in performance. This is exactly what Alexander himself does.

> ❝ *The second part* of the puzzle is how you act on that advice going forward. And that's something that I try to formulate and then once again I seek their advice. You know, really practical ways of implementing some of the changes.

Alexander may welcome the advice of his team, but he is unwaveringly conscious of the fact that he is the one who ultimately has to deliver on the day.

> ❝ *I think it's* great as an athlete to take control of your own career. Some people are daunted by that and

found that and I've found a good core group of people and essentially we discuss everything. I apply the same tough standards to everyone else as I apply to myself. So when someone gives me a suggestion I grill them on it. 'Why is that better?' 'How are we going to implement that?' 'How is that going to work in a practical sense?'

It's almost like a pop quiz. It's the same way when I was studying to be a physio and I would go to get a massage. I wouldn't tell the massage therapist where I was sore, I wanted to test them out. That's my personality – I wanted to see how good they were. It's similar with the people that I work with. I try and test them everyone now and again because it keeps them on their toes. It's the same way that I get tested and evaluated in races. Ninety-nine per cent of the time they come through in spades.

The one thing I've done very well is get great help. Some of that is good management and a lot of that is good luck – coming into contact with the right people at the right time, and I've been very lucky. But I do outsource a lot. I think that the minute you think you know everything, you're kidding. It's great to get an independent and arbitrary opinion that is a little bit removed from yourself – there's a lot of benefit in that, I've found. But the challenge is getting good people around you.

want a coach and want someone who tells them what to do. I like to be in control, I'm not a control freak by any stretch of the imagination but essentially it's my career, my livelihood and I feel a massive responsibility because it impacts on myself and my family. That doesn't mean that I can't trust other people because I do – I have a good team around me and I delegate and I don't look over anyone's shoulder or second guess. But ultimately I think it's very empowering to be the guy making the final decision.

As you have more success and other things in life become a factor, like family, you need to delegate more and outsource more and that's fine. The challenge then becomes finding people who are good. I have

At best, if you utilise the knowledge base of trusted and respected third-party peers then you will learn new things about yourself and gain an insight into different training techniques and strategies. At worst, you will learn nothing at all. In that scenario you have lost nothing, and are in the same position that you would have otherwise found yourself having not consulted with anyone. In short, building a 'team' around you can be an invaluable training aide and one that makes you a stronger, smarter athlete.

No man is an *island*

TODD WELLS

The vast majority of endurance events are individual pursuits. When the athlete crosses the line a single medal is handed out, the history books record one time (and one name), and in the case of the winners there is one person that everyone wants to interview. However, speak to any elite endurance athlete and they will tell you that being able to compete – and win – an event requires a team behind them that are essential in helping to propel them (hopefully) to glory.

In some instances, a large part of the team is the family and friends that an athlete surrounds themselves with. But there are sports that demand much more than simple emotional support. To be the best some athletes are dependent upon a team of specialists who are an integral part of them reaching the finish line.

American mountain biker Todd Wells has enjoyed an impressive career. A three-time Olympian (Athens, Beijing and London), Wells has claimed numerous US National Championships in both mountain biking and cyclo-cross. But arguably his most impressive wins came in 2011 at two of the biggest, and toughest, races on the endurance mountain-bike calendar. First Wells won the Leadville 100 MTB, a high-altitude, high-octane 100-mile 'race across the sky'. Wells took the win in 6 hours, 23 minutes and 28 seconds, the second fastest time in the history of the event (more than five minutes faster than Lance Armstrong's 2009 time over the same course). The American then set his sights on the multi-day, multi-stage La Ruta de los Conquistadores. A three-day race,

below Todd Wells has conquered some of the world's toughest mountain bike races.

the legendary La Ruta winds its way across the 161-mile width of Costa Rica, 'enjoying' almost 23,000 feet/7000 metres of vertical climbing en route to the finish line. On unfamiliar territory in a notoriously gruelling event and at his first attempt, Wells claimed victory in 17 hours, 18 minutes and 6 seconds. It was an outstanding race and one that served to enhance his already formidable reputation in endurance mountain-bike circles.

It was also brilliantly executed. Like so many endurance events, until recently La Ruta was a cult race on the mountain-bike calendar that attracted core, hardened cyclists. When Wells, who had been plying his trade on the professional UCI mountain-bike circuit, turned his attention to La Ruta, he decided to do so with the same intensity and preparation as he would for a world cup or world championship event.

above There are a lot of things that can go wrong in a mountain bike race.

❛❛**Having never been** to that event before, I did as much research as possible so I knew exactly what I was getting into. I talked to everybody that I could think of who had raced the event and I went down there with more than enough support.

With a race like La Ruta there's a lot of things that could go wrong mechanically. In some parts of Costa Rica there are no road signs to help you get to the assistance zones, so you need people who know where they are going. Even then we had two vehicles with all sorts of spares and bottles, and I had four people helping me.

Once Wells had made the decision to approach the event from a professional perspective, he called on the services of his team.

> **At the UCI events** I have a big team – the global Specialized team. We have probably the best team out there, the best mechanics, the equipment is always perfect and we're completely dialled in. I took that approach and brought it to a race like La Ruta, where a lot of times the locals have the advantage. Oftentimes, when a foreigner goes down there they might not have the budget or resources to approach that race from a top level. I feel like any race I want to do well in I approach like that.

Needless to say, even though Wells was the man riding the bike, every member of the team was called upon to help him successfully complete the race.

> **Each night,** after a stage they would spend about four hours redoing the bike. They would totally strip it down, look at all the parts that needed to be replaced, go through all the bearings, the cables, housing – it was a complete overhaul. It meant that when I got to the starting line the bike was in perfect condition.
>
> We had two cars and they would leapfrog each other to go into the different assistance zones where they would be there with bottles and all the spare parts in case I needed some type of assistance in those zones. There are four zones out on the course during each stage of La Ruta, and they were in the car all day driving to and from these zones, providing support. When I finished they would take the bike and they really make sure everything is taken care of so all I have to think about is the racing.

Of course, Todd Wells was undoubtedly helped on his way to victory by his Specialized team. But the confidence this team inspired in the American enabled him to ride his bike to the finish line on what is one of the world's toughest mountain-bike courses. The combination of a solid team environment and a focused ride helped Wells to realise his goals.

Building a solid team on trust and *respect*

The importance of having a solid team around you is echoed by both professional and amateur athletes across the sporting spectrum. Dee Caffari, the first woman to sail solo around the world in both directions, is acutely aware of the role that her team plays in both the preparation and execution of her record-breaking sailing attempts. 'Nothing I do happens without the team around me. Whether that's down to nagging about diet or going to the gym, or whether it's the boat team pushing me to go out for extra days on the water for training. I set the scene for what I want to achieve and they are basically there trying to keep me on the programme and not let me slip off.

> **There's always** the media person who will be there writing the stories, talking to the press and making sure that I do the interviews at the right time. There's the boat project manager who advises me on the technical side so should something break or I need to check something or fix something then he knows exactly what is on the boat, what spares I'm carrying and will help me administer the repairs. And then there's the project manager who puts the project together, deals with the sponsor and myself, and in my case that happens to be my partner. So he has the double whammy of having to keep the sponsor happy and dealing with the more emotional side of me.

Like Caffari, when Rachael Cadman undertook her successful attempt to become the first woman to complete the Enduroman Arch to Arc, she wanted her partner to be one of the members of the team that would be supporting her on the journey.

> **Because I knew** that I would be emotional, I wanted people who were calming. My fiancé and my fiancé's father are both quite steady and they are not overly emotive so I knew that that would be okay.

They were with me when I did my 10-hour swim and so they knew what feeding I needed, how I was going to feel if I had a really difficult time. All that stuff they knew how to deal with because they had already seen it and that was very important. The other person I had with me was Eddy who is the Enduroman director and he was the first person to complete the Arch to Arc so he had seen it all before and had loads of experience.

We didn't want anything massive. Some people get caught up in having huge groups of people and I think

that's quite hard because sometimes you need to say 'leave me alone' and that's quite difficult if you have to put on a public face. I knew I already had the media stuff to do and thought that would be enough pressure doing a media phase on top of a family phase so kept the whole thing really small.

Cadman, Caffari, Wells and Alexander have all identified people who can help them to realise their aims and ambitions. They have developed different relationships with different individuals, all possessing specific skill sets. They have done that because they have come to realise that their performances will be significantly

below A good team is an essential asset for any athlete.

enhanced by the help and support of the people that they trust and respect. So while history might only record the names of these athletes when it reflects on their achievements, they are all keen to point out the importance of the people they have around them before, during and after an event.

Endurance sports are physically and mentally demanding activities. Placed in the context of the 'real' world, where people have jobs and families and friends, those demands are even greater. Finding a balance in the lifestyle and calling on the advice and guidance of individuals that you know and respect are key ingredients to maximising performance potential. It is not easy, but with hard work and focus it is possible.

THE TEAM: KEY POINTS

- A happy athlete is a fast athlete. Achieve balance in your home/work/social life and your training will benefit.
- Use training partners as advisors. Seek their feedback on your strengths and weaknesses and consult with them on training strategies.
- Behind every winning athlete is a solid team. Use your team and call on them for help if it will enable you to realise your goals.
- Select a team that complements your racer's personality. You in race mode is different to you at home. Not everyone will appreciate that so select the personalities in your race-day team carefully.

below Remember: your racer's personality may be different from your everyday personality.

6

Control:
The management of the self

In all aspects of endurance sports – in fact, in all aspects of life – one of the key determinants between those who are successful and those who are not is the ability to take control. Not over everything – that is impossible. But over the things that the individual can directly control. In particular, how they control their approach and response to situations.

Controlling the *controllables*

Controlling the controllables is not only a key mantra in sports psychology but is employed throughout the business world too. The basic premise is that the individual cannot control an outcome, but can control the steps taken towards realising that outcome. For instance, you can control both the amount and intensity of the training that you do. However, you cannot control whether that training is enough to win a race – there are factors beyond your control that will ultimately decide that. Similarly, you can prepare your body for racing in extraordinary levels of cold or heat. However, you cannot control what the weather is doing on any given day and so that preparation may not equate to success.

It is ultimately the athlete who focuses on – and learns to take control over – the things that he or she can directly influence and change (the controllables) who is more likely to experience success at their chosen sport.

Learning to control the controllables is a quasi-holistic approach to training and racing that will shape every aspect of your athletic development. However, it is through its execution on race day that you will see the most ostensible benefits. Endurance races are long and they are hard. Often, they take place in extreme environments or climates and, frequently, athletes are heavily dependent upon equipment or machinery (bikes, boats, etc.). These factors provide plenty of things that can – and sometimes do – go wrong. And while none of us can legislate for mechanical failure, an unseasonably hot day or an irregularity in trail or road conditions, we can control our responses to unforeseen variables and so try to determine a positive outcome to potentially adverse situations.

Controlling the controllables manifests itself in many different ways during the training and racing cycle. To clarify what it means to be in control

Craig
ALEXANDER

❝ Preparation is the cornerstone of confidence, which in turn is the cornerstone of success. You know what you're training for and you prepare accordingly physically and mentally. A level of calm comes from knowing that you've done that.

above The 'marginal gains' approach of Team Sky looks at all possible controllables for improvement.

of these different variables, below are a few examples of how you can affect control over changing circumstances.

CONTROLLABLES IN COMPETITION

If you have established your 'A' race goals, what are the numbers that you have to hit in training in order to realise those goals? If you are racing to win, what are your opponents' strengths and weaknesses? How do they match up to your strengths and weaknesses? Once you know that information (which you can glean by doing some basic race-day homework), you can start to develop a training plan that will help drive you towards your goal. Of course, there is no legislating for what your opponents are doing – no athlete can control that. But by familiarising yourself with both the demands of your 'A' race and your opposition, you can develop a strategy that will best equip you to meet your competition objectives.

CONTROLLABLES IN THE BODY

Injuries are a frustrating and sometimes inevitable part of endurance sports. A carefully managed return from injury can, depending on time, mean that goals set at the start of the season can still be met. What's more, picking up an injury doesn't mean the end of training. Is there anything that you can do to maintain fitness during the recovery period? When you return to training, what sort of exercises should you do before adding significant volume? What exercises can you do to help ensure that there is no recurrence of the injury?

Sometimes the road back from injury is not easy. However, you can control elements of that road. There are plenty of historical examples across the sporting spectrum of athletes who have expedited their recovery by careful management of a potentially serious injury and gone on to realise their original goals for the year.

CONTROLLABLES IN THE MIND

If you practise endurance sports for long enough, there is a good chance that at some point you will experience a period of underperformance. The question to address is: why is it happening? To work this out, it is helpful to analyse all aspects of your preparation (from training to nutrition to rest periods and predefined targets). Somewhere there will be a shortfall. Once that shortfall has been addressed and work begins to rectify it, you can start to recover your form. As well as locating and addressing these performance shortfalls, it is important to maintain positive motivation and drive, even when it can be difficult to do so. As we discuss in Chapter 9 (Positivity: Whether you think you can or you can't, you're right), feelings and thoughts have a direct impact on physical performance. Mastering them is essential to being able to pull yourself out of that dip.

above The best athletes are those who focus only on their own performance.

CONTROLLABLES IN TECHNIQUE

Only the very best athletes have near-perfect technique (and even then some of them could theoretically improve), and so managing training and racing during periods of technique transition is essential. Technique changes occur for one very simple reason: to become a better athlete. However, this takes time (sometimes much longer than originally anticipated). During this transition period you can usually train and race without major issue, but there is a chance that your performances will fall below their previous levels. At this juncture, you need to stay focused on the long-term goal behind this change in technique, rather than the short-term dip in performance. How you mentally react to this kind of period will have a direct impact on your performance and motivation, and as such it is essential that you approach these transition periods with the correct mindset. For more on this see Chapter 9 (Positivity: Whether you think you can or you can't, you're right).

In many respects, controlling the controllables is akin to a theory expounded by the performance director of British Cycling, Sir Dave Brailsford. During the London 2012 Olympics, Brailsford spoke about the aggregation of marginal gains – looking for minimal improvements across the board, then bringing them together and seeing a significant improvement in performance

overall. Of course Brailsford, who during his tenure with British Cycling has overseen unprecedented levels of success, primarily looked for improvements in the competitive form and conditioning of his cyclists, but he also took a more holistic view and analysed every aspect of their lives. As he told the BBC during the London 2012 Olympics:

> ❝ *There are other things* that might seem on the periphery, like sleeping in the right position, having the same pillow when you are away and training in different places. Do you really know how to clean your hands? Without leaving the bits between your fingers? If you do things like that properly, you will get ill a little bit less. They're tiny things but if you clump them together it makes a big difference.

Theoretically, controlling the controllables sounds like a relatively straightforward concept. However, it is such an all-encompassing approach to sports performance that you can make it as complex and detailed or as simple and clear as you like. Only you can determine the level of control that you feel comfortable taking, and then determine how to apply that control to a sporting environment. As we are about to see, one man who has done that with almost unprecedented levels of success is three-time Ironman World Champion Craig Alexander.

Taking control of his *career*
CRAIG ALEXANDER

Three-time Ironman World Champion Craig Alexander has carved a formidable – and well-earned – reputation for being one of the most hard-working, dedicated men in triathlon. He is also renowned for being one of the most well-prepared athletes in the sport, and has been able to dominate the competition as a result. That preparedness comes from an intrinsic focus on – and belief in – the quality of his preparation, rather than the ability of the athletes he is competing against.

> ❝ *You watch the results* all year. A lot of the top guys have raced each other for a decade so we know each other's strengths and weaknesses. What is important is to watch patterns of athletes and how their form has progressed throughout the year: are they in great form; are they struggling a little bit; are they building towards the Ironman World Championships?
>
> Be aware of that, but essentially focus on the things that you can control, which is in effect your own preparation. Make sure you're in your best physical and mental shape for the biggest race of the year – that's always first base. If you can take care of that you're a long way to a successful outcome.

This measured approach is symptomatic of Alexander's attitude throughout his career. The Australian's introduction to triathlon was unconventional. Unlike many of his peers, Alexander didn't compete in his first race until the age of 21. He knew plenty about the sport already, having watched Australians Greg Welch and Michellie Jones dominating their respective fields, but he had never raced an event. Instead, he was a soccer player for 13 years (as well as an accomplished runner and swimmer), only taking up triathlon when a mate persuaded him to give it a go.

right 'Make sure you're in the best physical and mental shape for the biggest race of the year' – Craig Alexander

❝ A friend of mine from university suggested I do it – he was a good bike rider. He was in my house one day and saw I had some trophies for schoolboy swimming and athletics. I knew he had done a few triathlons and had asked him about them and he said he could help me out. I bought a bike from classifieds in the newspaper on a Thursday and did my first race on a Sunday.

With a natural aptitude for the sport, Alexander threw himself into it and quickly began to realise impressive levels of success.

❝ I didn't know anything, but I was studying to be a physiotherapist so I knew a little bit about physiology and the principles of endurance training – that kind of thing. But I had no coach so I was getting sessions out of magazines. I was training really hard and I progressed quite rapidly to the point where I was getting invited to go to national team training camps. There I came in contact with great athletes like Greg

above Positive self-affirmation.

Welch and a few others and I saw what the best in the world were doing.

I always felt I could make a career out of it. As a young boy I always wanted to be a professional athlete and I saw this as my pathway to it. I know it's crazy to say it like that as I was 21 years of age – when you conjure up images of elite athletes or endurance athletes, you think of people starting off in school. But for me, I started in my twenties and was a full-time university student but I had a good work ethic, I was very dedicated.

Alexander took control of his career early on. Compared to many of his peers, the Australian had arrived late to the sport. But while he saw that as a disadvantage at the time (he now concedes that it is probably the secret to his longevity – at the age of 38 he became the oldest man to win the Ironman World Championships in 2011), he did not let it deter him. In fact, it had quite the opposite effect and motivated him to work harder. Alexander believed that he needed to do the time before realising his goal: consistency in winning performances:

❝ I like to use the analogy of golf. Improving from someone who is a 20 handicap to say a single figure handicap – you can make that improvement pretty rapidly. But once you are at an 8 or 9 handicap, to get to scratch and become a pro – that last 10 per cent – that takes years. And that's what happened. Obviously I have physical gifts – I'm physically and genetically predisposed to do well at this sport. I have good biomechanics so I haven't been injured too much – I've worked a lot at that. But going from nothing to doing serious training and having a serious attitude – wanting to work hard – I think I got to a world-class level quite quickly. That fooled a lot of people. I was nowhere near the level to win those races physically.

As well as developing physically, Alexander began to work out the different psychological aspects of top-level sports performance that he needed to control if he was to achieve his goals. The first step was for him and his wife

ขึ้นจักรยาน
BIKE MOUNT

to dedicate their lives to his pursuit, basing themselves where the Australian would have the best chance of realising his ambitions. As such, these days – as they have been doing for many years – the Alexander family relocates for four months of the year from their home in Sydney, Australia to Boulder, Colorado in the USA. A mecca for triathletes, Boulder offers Alexander the best possible training environment as he builds towards the Ironman World Championships. Of course, with two young children, this upheaval isn't always easy. However, rather than having a negative impact on Alexander's psyche, he instead turns it into positive motivation.

" **I'm obviously not** the only one who sacrifices here and that's not lost on me. I think that's where the motivation comes from too. A lot of people around me are making sacrifices. My wife has put her career on hold as an emergency nurse, my daughter has to be home-schooled for four months of the year,

above In any endurance race there are many variables that have to be dealt with.

grandparents don't see their grandkids, our kids don't see their cousins or aunties and uncles: there are lots of sacrifices being made. So it's easy for me to say, 'You know what, I really appreciate that and I'm thankful for it and I'm not going to let anyone down and certainly do everything I can.' I don't have to win to repay them, but it's the very least I can do to prepare to the absolute optimum of my capabilities to repay them.

At the start of every season Alexander works out his goals for the coming year. For the most part, he has two target races: the September Ironman 70.3 World Championships (1.9km swim, 90km bike, 21.1km run) and October's Ironman World Championships (3.9km swim, 180km bike, 42.2km run) in Kona, Hawaii. He has won both races

(70.3 in 2006 and 2011; Ironman in 2008, 2009, 2011), and in 2011 became the first man to win both the 70.3 and Ironman World Championships in the same year. It is worth noting that in 2011 the World Triathlon Corporation changed the scheduling of the 70.3 World Championships from three weeks after Hawaii to four weeks before it (the conditions and course in Las Vegas was not entirely dissimilar to Hawaii, whereas the previous course was entirely different). This meant that is was viable for athletes to be competitive at both championships rather than be disadvantaged in one or the other.

Of course, Alexander races other events apart from the two world championships. However, by and large these events serve as tune-up races – although he will aim to peak for the one full-distance Ironman race that he has to enter before Kona to validate his Hawaii slot.

Like any professional athlete, Alexander develops a training plan that is built around peaking for his 'A' races. As discussed in Chapter 4, this plan is carefully constructed around the areas of his performance that both he and his team identify as needing the most work. Needless to say, despite seeking the advice of those that he trusts, Alexander is ultimately the one who oversees and executes the training plan. In that way he retains complete control over his athletic development, and can manipulate his training to suit the areas of performance that he feels needs the most work. Having enjoyed a long career as a professional athlete – and a champion of his sport – Alexander has honed the elements of his training to give him the best possible chance of success during competition.

That's not to say that he has always got things right. In fact, he readily accepts that this is not the case, and he has learnt from the mistakes that he has made during his career. This willingness to learn and change is yet another reason why he has forged a long career at the top of his sport.

❝ **2009 was a tough race** and a tough lesson in Kona because I felt a pressure to replicate everything identically to the year before. From race schedule to

training to the final lead-up days. I think that was a bit of inexperience and a bit of nerves and I over-trained. I cooked myself big time. I fainted three weeks before the race in Kona from heat stroke out there. But I was able to defend my title and I think that was more attributable to mental toughness and a desire to put up a worthy title defence.

Even as a multiple world champion you still succumb to nerves and make silly mistakes and I think I learnt a lot and I matured as an athlete after that because I learnt that everything didn't have to be the same. It just had to be the best that it could be for that set of circumstances. It was a good learning experience and I was able to get the win and it was a very satisfying win because it was an ugly win – I hurt all day.

And obviously when I say I wasn't in great physical shape – when you hear elite athletes say that you're talking in percentage points – 1 per cent of 1 per cent – that's what you're talking about. And that's the difference at that level. But I knew for some reason my form had peaked about four weeks before that race in 2009. So my form had started to slowly come off the boil a little bit and I panicked and overdid it.

Alexander's entire season is built around controllables. From location to training to race selection and, of course, attitude and motivation, the Australian has learnt valuable lessons and mastered the art of taking charge of his own career. What's more, in terms of racing this approach enables him to adapt and change his strategy – and indeed his strengths – as the season unfolds.

At no time in his career has this been called to the fore more than in 2011. If Alexander managed to tough out his win at Kona in 2009 after 'overcooking' his preparation, he was caught in the Ironman equivalent of a pincer movement in 2010 that led him to surrender his Kona crown and completely re-evaluate his training and racing strategy.

During the 2010 World Championships, Alexander was subjected to an unprecedented and sustained series of 'attacks' from some of the strongest bikers in the sport as they attempted to weaken the then world champion going into the marathon. The Australian finished fourth on a tough day in Hawaii in a time of 8:16:53. In one of the tightest races in recent years, he was 6 minutes and 16 seconds behind the winner, Chris McCormack. Alexander had swum and ran faster than his fellow Australian, but lost 7 minutes and 44 seconds to McCormack on the bike.

> *It was a tough defeat.* It was no secret that a lot of the top guys got together before the race and conspired to form an alliance, and that hurt me. It felt like it was a team race, but again it made me a better athlete because they didn't break the rules. They came up with a game plan and it showed me up a little bit. Maybe it showed that I was a little bit one dimensional – I'd always typically swum with the leaders and then conserved a lot on the bike and waited for the marathon and then that had been enough. They showed flaws in that strategy.

> It hurt me for a while and then after a while I learnt that it wasn't personal, that that is just sport and that that is just human nature. As I said it was a great lesson because it made me a better athlete and it made me win in a different way the following year.

It certainly did. Alexander turned a negative experience into positive motivation and went away to work on his bike strength. When he returned to Hawaii in October

below Alexander has been able to turn adversity into success during his career, after learning some tough lessons.

2011 he surprised the triathlon world with a dominant victory capped off by an outstanding 4 hour, 24 minutes and 5 seconds bike split – a significant improvement on his 4 hours, 39 minutes and 35 seconds from 2010. It was the fifth fastest bike split in the history of the race and helped propel him to the finishing line in a course record of 8:03:56.

For an athlete of Alexander's ability to register such a significant increase in speed on the bike is a testament of his perspective on training and racing.

> ❝ **It's about improving** every year. That's where the motivation comes from, it's very simple. And being a better athlete. There are always things that you can do in a sport like Ironman to improve. Obviously the steep part of the improvement curve is long gone but you're looking for the one percenters, as the football coaches call them – the little half-percentage increments here and there. At the highest level of any sport it is usually a big investment of time and effort and energy to get little

above 'Preparation is the cornerstone of confidence, which in turn is the cornerstone of success' – Craig Alexander

incremental improvements but that's what you're after and it's exciting when you see those improvements.

The development of Craig Alexander as a competitor between 2010 and 2011 is the perfect example of an athlete taking control of his strategy and executing that strategy on the day. Alexander could have easily let the experience of 2010 overshadow his preparations for 2011 and simply gone back to Hawaii's Big Island with a similar race-day strategy in the hope that lightning wouldn't strike twice. It would have been a fair assumption given that Chris McCormack, who won the world championship in 2010 and who was widely credited for being the instigator of the strategy to weaken Alexander, took time away from the long-distance triathlon in 2011. However, rather than leave the World Championships to chance, the Australian took control of the situation and changed significant aspects of his preparation in a bid to realise a positive result. He controlled his reaction to adversity and emerged a stronger athlete as a result. This is typical of the way that he controls his approach to sport as a whole.

" *I focus on myself* – the things I can control. I hear sports psychologists all the time saying control the controllables – forget the weather, everything else. And it's true: you can't burn energy or stress about things that are out of your control. You certainly need to give due diligence to a lot of things – like the weather – that all play a part in a performance, particularly in a race like Kona. You need to know the prevailing conditions, whether the trade winds will be blowing and where they will be blowing from. You can't be ignorant to those facts and that's part of being a professional as well: making sure that every little detail has been given its due diligence. But you can't worry about things either. You can't say 'Oh, it's going to be 40°C and the humidity is 90 per cent.' You can't worry about it, you prepare for it.

Like I say, preparation is the cornerstone of confidence, which in turn is the cornerstone of success. You know what you're training for and you prepare accordingly, physically and mentally. A level of calm comes from knowing that you've done that.

Craig Alexander is an exceptional athlete on many levels. At the core of his strategy is a relatively simple approach to training and racing that can be employed by any athlete, regardless of the level at which they are competing. Controlling the controllables is about focusing on – and managing – the things that you can directly impact. From physical effort to emotional response, it is important to focus on the variables that you can manage and that will directly impact your performance. If you can do that then you will ultimately channel that focus into improved performance, and so stand a better chance of realising your objectives.

above Do not waste energy worrying about things that are out of your control.

CONTROL: KEY POINTS

- Focus only on the situations and outcomes that you can control.
- Control the controllables in all aspects of your life: from racing to training to recovery to work/family situations.
- Prepare the body and mind for every eventuality on race day and you will overcome issues and obstacles faster and with more clarity.
- Acknowledge and learn from your mistakes. Let them turn you into a stronger athlete.

7

Focus:
Managing the here and now

When a musician starts to play his or her instrument, or a writer starts to write, they focus solely on what they are doing in that very moment. They are not thinking about the end of the song. Nor do they think about the words that they wrote just a few paragraphs ago. They are completely and utterly focused on the moment that they are in. They need that level of focus to perform their art to the best of their abilities.

The act might be different, but the importance of complete and utter focus in the sporting arena is the same. Professional athletes are, for the most part, masters at focusing. Of course, some are able to focus better over prolonged periods of time than others. But that is usually one of the determining factors between the very good and the very best. The best can block out every thought and every distraction and focus purely on what they are doing then and there. Sydney Olympic Gold medallist Cathy Freeman once spoke about a 'bubble of silence' when she ran. Even with the weight of a nation's expectation on her shoulders and at a home Olympics, she didn't hear the crowd until she had crossed the finish line. The Australian was completely and utterly focused on the execution of her race strategy.

Attaining that level of focus is not, however, an easy thing to do.

It is an easy thing to practise though. It is as simple as sitting down in a comfortable chair and looking at an object. It can be any object. Look at it, clear your mind of any other thoughts and focus solely on it. Try to hold that focus for as long as possible without any other thoughts creeping into your mind. At the beginning of this sort of exercise it is usually a matter of seconds until you start thinking about other things. But the more you practise, the longer your ability to focus on one thing will be.

Of course, there is a pretty sizeable difference between being able to focus on a static object when sitting comfortably and being able to focus your mind on physical activity when mentally fatigued. And if the ability to focus for more than a few seconds on a pot plant takes a little time and effort to develop, then focusing during exercise takes even more so. However, the principles remain the same: the athlete is looking to be centred on the now. They are focusing on managing their body and mind through the sporting activity as it unfolds. That does not mean reflecting on a missed feed or a target time that has slipped by. Nor does it entail getting overly confident

Dean **KARNAZES**

" Just focus on being present and not thinking about anything other than the here and now. That's really how I keep going through these things. It's almost a discipline to do that for eight, ten or twelve hours at a time, but that's how I do it.

when you are up on your splits and starting to think about the end of the race. It means dealing with the reality of the race as it is unfolding. It means focusing on technique, listening to your body and its needs, and concentrating on executing your race strategy.

Doing that requires harnessing many of the principles that we outline throughout this book, from controlling the controllables (Chapter 6) to visualisation (Chapter 8) to turning negative self-talk into a positive affirmation of ability (Chapter 9), you can call on various psychological strategies to help you realise the optimum conditions for focus on your performance.

below Focus necessitates complete control over your mind.

Improving your *focus*

There are also things that you can do to improve your focus both before and during exercise. For instance:

BEFORE – RELAX

Relaxation prior to athletic performance is different from conventional explanations of relaxation. It is not a case of slowing everything down and being completely calm. Rather, it is about channelling the adrenalin and the nerves into a positive outcome. As we will see in Chapter 9, physiological performance is directly related to mood, and an athlete that is in a positive mindset will generally perform better than a highly strung athlete. Saying that, some athletes do thrive on nervous energy. Either way,

the key for any athlete is to identify the triggers that enable them to realise that ideal mental state. Those triggers could be anything from breathing to music to pre-race exercises. Whatever they are, an athlete should work to identify those triggers and then use them to ensure that their mind and body is ready to compete.

BEFORE – PREPARE

Confidence comes from preparation, and if you have hit your numbers in training, then you can go into the race confident that you are able to perform at your desired level on the day. If, however, you have under-prepared, then you are more likely to dwell on this lack of preparation, and that could easily turn into negative emotion when fatigue kicks in.

DURING – FOCUS ON FORM

You've probably read articles on how to execute the perfect swim stroke or the correct technique for running. Now is the time to focus on that. Try to 'watch' what the body is doing and correct any technical shortfall. This will ultimately make you a faster athlete.

DURING – USE KEYWORDS OR MANTRAS

Many top athletes use keywords to help them through difficult times. From counting up to 100 to repeating a word (or words) over and over, the mind becomes focused on what the body is doing and is distracted from fatigue.

DURING – LISTEN TO YOUR BREATHING

This simple strategy can help you to stay focused on the here and now if you find your mind starting to wander. We all tend to have a particular rhythm of breathing when we swim, cycle, run or whatever else. That rhythm of breathing is often linked to a stroke, stride or a pedal turn. If you focus on that breathing then you are channelling your thought processes into your actions, and so focusing directly on your performance.

DATEV

The best athletes compete in a 'bubble of silence', and can be completely oblivious to what is going on around them.

DURING – BE PRESENT IN YOUR SURROUNDINGS

This might sound counter-intuitive, but one of the many positives of endurance sports is the fact that they often take place in remarkable environments. There is no harm in being present in that environment and being part of the world around you. Obviously, it's not ideal for your mind to completely wander off and start daydreaming, but you can certainly take time to notice where you are and what you are doing as you are doing it. After all, for the vast majority of athletes, endurance sports are a pastime rather than a profession.

Control the things you can *control*

As well as effective techniques to centre the mind on athletic performance, the key to focusing is to be in control of your own race. Do not worry about things that have happened or that might happen, instead focus on controlling the body and mind as the race unfolds (this is examined in more detail in Chapter 6 – Control: The management of the self). For instance, it is no good thinking about the end of a race unless, of course, you are very close to it. Neither is it useful to focus on the actions of an opponent (unless you are in direct competition), the intervention of an official, or situations that have occurred previously in the race. There is nothing that you can do about these incidences, and the more energy that you expend focusing on them, the more it is likely to impair your performance. Instead, where possible turn adverse or negative situations into positives. Remember to maintain focus on your technique, your mood (engaging in positive self-talk, as discussed in Chapter 9 – Positivity: Whether you think you can or you can't, you're right), nutrition and hydration, and your race-day strategy. These are all things that can have a direct, positive impact on the outcome of a race, and will ultimately help you to achieve your goals.

Living in the *moment*
DEAN KARNAZES

One man who expounds the importance of racing in the here and now is ultra-marathon runner Dean Karnazes. A pioneer in his sport, Karnazes rediscovered his love for running in an unlikely place.

> **I had hung up** my shoes after high school, and then on my thirtieth birthday I was out with some friends and I decided at 11 o'clock that night to go for a run. I thought: 'I'm going to run 30 miles to celebrate my thirtieth birthday.' I was really bored with my life. There was no intensity, there was no struggle – I was a corporate executive. I had gone to school, then graduate school and then I went to business school and I had a really cushy job but I was extremely bored. So that night I walked out of the bar – I hadn't run for ten years – and I ran 30 miles.

Of course, it wasn't the first time that Karnazes had run. A prodigious runner as a child, the American had carved out a solid reputation at high school, winning the prestigious California State One Mile Race and competing in numerous events throughout his school years. Then life got in the way. As so often happens with young talent, Karnazes followed the well-worn path through school and university, and found himself working a desk job.

The epiphany that followed his thirtieth birthday was profound and life-changing. Of course, Karnazes didn't go into work the next day and resign. But that 30-mile run, and the enjoyment that he took from it, had planted a seed that changed the way he approached his life.

> **I'd get up** at four o'clock in the morning and I'd train really hard before work. And then when I was on business meetings, instead of going out to lunch with everyone, I'd slip on my runners and go out for an hour and then take a sponge bath in the sink. My behaviour started varying quite a bit from my colleagues and then after five years I decided to do what I loved.

above Dean Karnazes (right)

Since walking away from the desk job Karnazes has not only carved out a reputation for taking on some quite extraordinary challenges, but has also tackled – and won – some of the classic races on the ultra-marathon circuit. In 2012 Karnazes completed the legendary Badwater Ultramarathon for the tenth time, having won the race once (2004). He has also completed the Western States 100-Mile Endurance Run 11 times, won the Vermont Trail 100 Mile Endurance Run and was the overall winner of the 4 Deserts series.

But while the successful completion of these races has helped cement his reputation in ultra-running circles, it is his 'larger' projects that have captured the attention of the mainstream media. Since 2004, Karnazes has overcome some quite remarkable challenges. After running 200 miles non-stop (in a race designed for relay teams), he went back to the same race a year later and ran 262 miles (or ten back-to-back marathons).

This inspired him to see how far he could run non-stop and, as detailed in Chapter 2, he reached his limits at 350 miles after 80 hours and 44 minutes of constant running. In addition to the 350 miles, Karnazes set himself the challenge of completing 50 marathons in 50 states in 50 days; has run across the USA from Anaheim to New York (3,000 miles in 75 days); and has run 148 miles in 24 hours on a treadmill. He has also raced on all seven continents on Earth. In so doing, Karnazes has pushed his body further than most people consider humanly possible, and tackled extremes of temperature, weather and race conditions.

The question most people ask is how he does it. Of course, some of his races take place at organised events. Many, however, do not. And when it is just Dean

Karnazes against the road or trail, how is it possible for him to stay motivated and keep on going?

❝ **When I've really analysed** what's going on it's almost like a Zen-like state. I've really had to put myself in the moment to be present there and then. It's so hard not to think about the future and not to think: 'Oh my God this run is really going to suck', 'I've only had two hours' sleep', 'I'm nauseous', 'I'm jetlagged'. Instead, just go through the motions. Put on your runners, lace up your shoes, open the door to the hotel ... you know, at every moment be present. Run down the stairs and just put one foot in front of the other. Literally get to that state where you're saying 'all I'm going to do next is put my next foot forward'. It's almost like a meditative state.

For Karnazes, the overall performance benefits of being able to focus completely on his performance are evident in his achievements. However, this focus also allows him to push through the difficult patches of a race or challenge.

❝ **When I hit** these low points I really get in the moment and try my best to take my next footstep better than my last. And just focus on being present and not thinking about anything other than the here and now. That's really how I keep going through these things. It's almost a discipline to do that for eight, ten or twelve hours at a time, but that's how I do it.

below Complete focus involves always staying in the moment.

This ability to focus completely on the here and now of his performance has allowed Karnazes to realise some quite exceptional feats. It is also a skill that he has learnt to utilise away from sport.

"*I live in the moment.* I think it's a transferable skill that I've learnt through endurance sports. For instance, for me writing is 1 per cent inspiration, 99 per cent perspiration. And when I write I really have to do the same thing: I have to be present. I'm so in the moment and I'm not thinking about anything else.

You have some of your clearest thoughts when you're not distracted by everything else that goes on in life. So that's how I get through difficult periods no matter what it might be – bereavement or any sort of struggle. If I can get in the moment it's really how I get through it.

When I look at certain races I do – for instance, the Western States 100 Mile – I've done it 11 times and I don't even know the course that well. Other racers go out and analyse every step of the 100 miles. They know where all the aid stations are, they know precisely the climbs. A lot of triathletes do that same thing – they go to Kona early and know the lava fields – but to me I can't remember. I'm like 'Why do all these other guys know the course so well? I've done it more than them.' And it's just because of that reason: I'm so in the moment I don't pay attention to anything except being here and now. So I don't really look around and see where I'm at and what's going on in the race, I'm just really present.

As well as helping Karnazes optimise his performance, he believes that this strategy is also the key to his continued passion for endurance sports – and ultra-marathon running in particular.

"*As soon as I start* to live and die by split times then I know I'm going to burn out. I'll never forget that there's one person – I won't mention the name but a very famous champion at Western States who has won it multiple times – and one year I passed this individual at

above For Karnazes, the hours of focus over the course of an ultra-marathon take discipline.

mile 95 of a 100-mile race. We were running through the Sierra Nevada mountains – a gorgeous mountain range – and were out in the wilderness crossing rivers and it was just fantastic, and I passed this individual and all he said to me was 'Where's Steve? Where's Steve? How far back is he?' He was wondering where the third-placed guy was. He didn't even care that he was out on this wilderness trail in the gorgeous outdoors – I don't think he saw a pine tree in the entire day! All he cared about was getting to the finish line first.

Needless to say he no longer runs at all – he hates running now. And when that happened I thought 'My God, this person's head is in so different – in another place than mine.'

Dean Karnazes's ability to focus over hours – and sometimes days – is quite exceptional. It is a trait that he shares with many top athletes, all of whom are able to train their mind on their goals. This ability not only keeps them motivated, but it means that they are able to register some quite outstanding performances. Karnazes's does so not only in the field of ultra-marathon running, but in all of the physical challenges that he sets himself.

Focusing on extrinsic *factors*

At the start of this chapter we discussed the importance of focusing, and being in control of a performance. However, there are occasions – and every athlete will experience them from time to time – when it is necessary to widen the scope of focus beyond just the performance and instead target an outcome or an external factor. Of course, the competitive athlete has to continue to focus on and manage their own performance, but in these circumstances they must also pay credence to factors outside of their personal sphere. Maintaining this dual focus allows the best athletes in the world to respond to the movements of their competition, and so realise their objectives (winning a race, hitting a target time, etc.).

As discussed in detail in Chapter 14, at the London 2012 Olympic Games Nicola Spirig was part of one of the closest finishes in triathlon history. With a kilometre to go Spirig, who suffered from stomach cramps throughout the race, began to increase the pace on the run in the hope of splitting the group she was running with. At that time, with her body being pushed to its limits, she had only one thing on her mind:

> ❝ *I couldn't think* about just winning a medal and not getting fourth because that would have meant that I was fighting for third or second and not about winning first and taking risks fighting for the Gold. So I really had to focus on Gold and I really had to think that it would be the only medal that I wanted, and I was willing to risk everything to win the Gold, and not just run for not getting a medal. I think that was really important for the win.

This drive for Gold propelled Spirig all the way home. When she crossed the line, timing chips couldn't separate her from Lisa Nordén and organisers were forced to determine the winner by a photo finish. Despite registering identical times, Spirig's torso was adjudged to have crossed the line ahead of Nordén's, and the Swiss woman was awarded Gold. If she hadn't been so focused on winning that Gold would she have still done so? We'll never know. Spirig, however, believes that that absolute focus on winning Gold was the key to her success.

Nicola Spirig's focus helped to drive her towards the Gold medal at the London 2012 Olympics. However, winning a medal or a race is not the only external factor that athletes need to focus on if they are to realise their pre-race goals.

Road cyclist George Hincapie forged a formidable reputation as being a man who could not only focus on his own performance, but on the performances of those around him. Road cycling is unlike many endurance sports in that the major races are, by and large, team events. Every team has a leader, and every leader is supported by *domestiques*. Despite being one of a number of riders who admitted to doping in 2012, Hincapie is still widely regarded as being one of the best, if not the best, *domestiques* that ever raced in the Grand Tours. Over the course of a 19-year career (itself an impressive feat), Hincapie raced in the Tour de France 15 times, won one stage outright and three Team Time Trial stages. He also registered wins at numerous other races, and competed in multiple Olympic Games. Hincapie's role, however, was not defined by personal victories. Rather, he was one of the key men in a team that would work for the victory of another athlete.

> ❝ *My gift was to* be one of the best *domestiques* ever. That was just to be able to shepherd around my leader in the peloton, know when to be at the front and know when to relax. That's what I was really good at. We were all class athletes but to win the Tour de France you really have to be a freak of nature. I knew that I couldn't do it, but the guys like Lance [Armstrong] and [Alberto] Contador and Cadel [Evans], they could. So for me to sacrifice a stage win or a result on one stage

to be able to help one of those guys be able to win the Tour was more important and more gratifying to me. It kind of defined my career.

Without a doubt, Hincapie earned the respect of the peloton because of his role working for those other men. He was the only cyclist to ride with Lance Armstrong in every one of his now erased seven Tour de France 'wins'. After Armstrong retired he went on to claim another two Tour de France 'victories', the first with Alberto Contador in 2007, the second with Cadel Evans in 2011.

The secret to Hincapie's success as a *domestique* was his ability to maintain a dual focus. In his role he had to focus not only on his own riding, but also that of his team leader and the competition. This is a skill that few riders possess, and one that demands absolute focus – and a willingness to sacrifice your own ambition from time to time.

> **The overall goal** was to protect the team leader at races like the Tour de France, but there were many stages where you could try and get in the breakaway to either put pressure on other teams to make them work more or to even go for your own result. So it really depended on what the strategy for the day was.

Of course, with plenty of stages in excess of 200 kilometres, strategies can, and frequently do, change. And that is where a cyclist with the knowledge and experience of Hincapie comes to the fore. These days the *directeur sportif* of a team (the person who manages the race-day strategy) is constantly monitoring the action from a team car that follows the peloton, and he or she is in constant communication with the riders. However, things change quickly in the peloton. Speeds are high (in 2011 Cadel Evans's average speed when he won the Tour de France was 39.78km/h over the course of a 3,430km race), and accidents or attacks are commonplace. As

right Sports like cycling require athletes to shift focus from their own performances to what is happening around them.

right George Hincapie built a career by being able to read races better than almost anyone else.

such, riders have to be ready to respond immediately to movements or incidents in the peloton, and more often than not someone in the team has to be prepared to make the tactical call.

> **You start with** a strategy but the strategy has to be varied throughout the circumstances that happened on the road. That was one of my strong points: I was able to make a lot of decisions on the road as the race was going on when the *directeur* in the car couldn't see what was happening. The team would look to me to make those calls.

Hincapie's ability to read a race was unquestionably a pivotal factor in his success at Grand Tour level. He was able to do this because of a deft understanding of race-day strategies, and the ability to focus both on his own performance and the performances of those around him. In this respect he was revered by the cycling community as being one of the best in the world.

The ability to focus is one of the key differentials between the very good and the very best in sport. The athletes who have carved significant reputations for themselves on the international stage are masters of the art of focusing. Primarily they will focus on their own performance and use that focus to do their best to realise a positive outcome. But at times, and in certain situations, they will also be able to turn their focus to external factors. Again, though, this technique is employed to give the athlete the best chance of realising a positive outcome.

Like professionals, amateur athletes undoubtedly benefit from working on their levels of focus. It is all too easy to get distracted by things like negative thoughts or external factors to the detriment of performance. By maintaining a focus on the execution of a performance, athletes can channel their energy into meeting the targets that they have set for themselves, targets that will ultimately propel them towards their goals.

FOCUS: KEY POINTS

- Focus on the moment. Do not berate or congratulate yourself too much or look too far ahead.
- Practise focus away from sport. See how long you can focus on a single object with a clear mind.
- Be present in the environment where you are training or competing. Look around and enjoy it – it will help to relax your mind.
- Determine a pre-race routine that prepares your body and mind for competition.
- Find key performance aides that help you to stay focused on your strategy during a race or training (e.g. repeat keywords or listen to your breathing patterns when exercising).

8

Visualisation:
Seeing is believing

William **TRUBRIDGE**

> ❝ I use visualisation to prepare for every dive. I visualise every aspect of it and what I need to do and get right. You're programming that information in there so that during the dive itself your body and everything works without you having to make decisions or rationalise things.

The world's best athletes often talk about the importance of visualisation. Visualisation helps them to focus their minds and prepare themselves for an upcoming race. Athletes visualise what they want to happen and how they will feel when it does.

Visualisation is a process that is commonly associated with producing mental images of a race or event as you ideally see it unfolding. However, athletes who are exceptional at the practice of visualisation will often engage additional senses, such as hearing, feeling and smell. In essence, some of the very best athletes in the world transport themselves into an ideal moment in their mind, and use every mental tool at their disposal to visualise the realisation of their goals.

Visualisation is not just confined to athletic performance. In fact, it is something that people do every day. Rather like daydreaming, people regularly visualise specific scenarios that they want to go 'right' – for instance, asking their boss for a raise or having an important conversation with their partner. Of course, the individual might not necessarily realise that they are visualising specific instances, but by mentally enacting how they want these scenarios to unfold – what the boss will say or how their partner will react to a conversation – they are beginning a process of visualisation that is not dissimilar to that performed by some of the world's best athletes. Successfully visualising a scenario has a dual impact on the individual: it motivates them to act and it relaxes them, which means that they are prepared for what might happen (in a best-case scenario, anyway).

In much the same way, visualisation is an essential part of sports performance. It helps many athletes push through difficult periods and prepares them to realise their ambitions. At the same time it helps channel an athlete's inevitable nervous energy (even international sports stars get nervous!), helping them to 'see' a race before it actually happens. Olympic sprinters, for instance, often talk about how visualisation helps their bodies and minds prepare for a big race. Before a race they will mentally rehearse everything from walking out into a packed, cheering stadium, to preparing their blocks, to the hush of the crowd before the start, to their reaction to the starter's gun, mentally 'running' through the phases of the race before crossing the finishing line in first place. This process excites them, it prepares them and it helps them to focus on what they are about to do.

Regardless of whether an athlete is competing in their first amateur race or third Olympic Games, the process and fundamentals of visualisation are the same. It is worth noting at this stage, though, that visualisation takes practice. Inevitably, some people are naturally adept at the process and can start to visualise specific race-day scenarios with astonishing ease. However, like racing itself, most people need time to work at visualisation before being able to use it effectively.

Effective **visualisation**

The first step for a novice athlete is to visualise something pleasant and 'easy'. For instance, close your eyes, try to clear your head of any other thoughts, and focus your mind on a lawn of freshly cut grass. What does the lawn look like? Is the grass a deep, vivid green or is it parched by the sun? How does it smell? Is the grass damp or is it dry? What does it feel like when you walk over it in bare feet? This is a pretty simple exercise, but in closing your eyes – and your mind – and focusing solely on the grass you are beginning to visualise an experience. Of course, you are calling on your personal recollections and memories to construct that experience, but that is one of the fundamental objectives of the exercise. For someone who finds visualisation difficult, it is essential to practise imagining everyday objects or things before working specifically on race-day scenarios. As with any pursuit, you start with the basics and work up to more complex imagery.

Once you feel you are able to clearly visualise the grass – or a chair, or anything else that engages your senses – it is time to put it into a sporting context. The key with the practical implementation of visualisation is to ensure that the performance you are visualising is successful. By successful, we mean that you are performing the technical aspects of the sport flawlessly and are on course to realising your goals. Again, keep it simple to start off

above Many pro athletes talk about the importance of visualisation.

with, and if it helps keep it slow motion (as you become more adept at managing the mind you can do this in real time). Simply imagine yourself swimming, cycling, running (or doing whatever else you choose to do). Your form is perfect, you are feeling strong, and you are in your favourite place. That's it. You are simply visualising the act of athletic performance.

How do you see yourself during these periods of visualisation? Is it from an internal or external perspective? For instance, when you are visualising are you looking through your own eyes or are you watching yourself from the outside, as if you were a spectator? It makes no real odds whether you visualise from an internal or external perspective, but it is something to be conscious of. More importantly: what are you visualising? Can you see only yourself or can you see your surroundings too? To what level of detail? Can you feel the ground beneath your feet? Can you smell the woods around you or the chlorine in the pool? The more specific the visualisation and the more you can engage your other senses, the better you will ultimately execute the task at hand.

As your control over the visualisation improves, so the scenarios that you are visualising should develop. If you are a runner, imagine yourself pushing through the pain barrier as you run down the finishing chute. If you are a cyclist, imagine going to your drops in the final sprint for the finishing line, or if you are a swimmer, try and visualise the last 100 metres of the push for home. As part of this visualisation you are being true to yourself: you know in your mind that every sinew of your body will be hurting. But sometimes pain is not a negative thing. In fact, in endurance sports, realising your goals is inevitably accompanied by a degree of suffering.

Again, keep the visualisations in slow motion to begin with, and slowly build up until you're performing in real time. As your visualisation skills improve, so the scenarios and race situations that you visualise should increase.

Hopefully, if you have had the time and practise to visualise your performance, then on race day you will feel relaxed, focused and ready to perform at your best. However, as with many aspects of endurance sports it is not always that simple. Unlike a 100-metre runner, who can visualise every phase of their race, it is almost impossible to visualise every aspect of an endurance event. For one thing, the time taken to do so is counter-productive. Also, in many races, the course is, to an extent, something of an unknown entity. However, it is possible in most – not all – instances to familiarise yourself with the key points of a race (a tough hill, a technical section, key turn markers). If you have the time and opportunity to familiarise yourself with those

elements you can then work on the visualisation of your performance on the day, and so you will be more confident when it comes to executing your race in a competitive situation.

Visualisation comes in many ways, shapes and forms. When practised and trained, it can undoubtedly be a useful tool for managing performance. However, the human mind is such that inevitably the individual and the athlete will, at times, experience negative visualisation. If, for instance, you are having a hard time in training and visualise yourself dropping out of a race, you will dramatically increase your chances of doing just that. In those scenarios it is important to identify where these negative thought patterns are coming from (deficiencies in training, overly ambitious goals, etc.) and how best to deal with them.

Many athletes use visualisation to focus their bodies and minds on realising their optimum performance. It is a skill that, like any sport, needs to be practised and honed before it is perfected (there are plenty of resources available that explore in-depth the application of visualisation in athletic performance). But when the athlete can visualise a strong performance in a specific race scenario, they will undoubtedly be well on their way to realising the execution of that performance come race day.

Visualisation and the professional *athlete*

Elite athletes are experts at ensuring that their minds are ready to push their bodies to perform. As we have already discussed, one of the ways that many of the best athletes in the world do this is by spending time visualising their actions during a race, and/or familiarising themselves with the event they are about to tackle. In endurance sports this is not always easy, and for many amateur athletes time constraints mean that it is almost impossible.

Ultra-runner Ryan Sandes is a strong advocate of visualisation. Where possible, Sandes will make every

effort to arrive at a race early with a view to acclimatising to conditions at an event and familiarising himself with a course.

> *Luckly, on a lot* of ultra-trail races – the 100-milers and 100-kilometre races – the course is pre-marked and you can pre-run sections of the course which makes a big, big difference. Just being able to know what is coming your way on race day, know which bits you can push hard on and know where your strengths and weaknesses are going to lie is a real help.
>
> I do a lot of visualisation and try to get a feel for the course. For Leadville I was out there a few weeks before the race and I got to run most of the course. That definitely helped me familiarise myself with the routes. On race day I could get absorbed by the surroundings and just focus. That way, I could almost take it as if it was just another long training run instead of being so focused on the race around me.

Sandes won the Leadville Trail 100 ultra-marathon in 2011, thanks in part to his preparation for the event and ability to visualise himself on certain sections of the race.

Visualisation and the *dive*
WILLIAM TRUBRIDGE

Running and triathlon are sports where visualisation is undoubtedly beneficial to managing the mind of the athlete with the goal of realising a successful outcome. However, it is not an essential tool for a runner, and the athlete can compete to a high level without employing visualisation techniques.

Freediving, however, is quite the opposite. It is a sport that demands perfect mind management, and visualisation is a common – if not universal – tool employed by the world's best freedivers. Admittedly, it is not your typical endurance sport. However, aside from the dangers – real or perceived – that are constantly

left William Trubridge prepares to dive.

present within the sport, a basic understanding of the impact of freediving upon the body is testament to the need of the athlete to attain absolute focus before a dive takes place. William Trubridge, world-record-holding freediver, explains:

> ❝ **There's a lot** that is going on in the body during a deep freedive. When we hold our breath the body goes into oxygen conservation mode. It shuts down the blood flow to the periphery so that your muscles and tissues work anaerobically and that conserves oxygen for the organs that can't survive without it: the heart, lungs and the brain. So your body is pushing the blood into the core to conserve that oxygen.
>
> The pressure is also acting on the air spaces so you have to equalise your ears. The lungs collapse to a size that would normally cause your ribcage to implode. But there's another effect where the blood vessels inside swell up with blood – they engorge – and that compensates for the loss of volume due to the pressure. So your lungs are drawing in this blood while the outside of your body is pushing it to the core and that increases the pressure in the core and consequentially your heart rate drops to maintain a steady level of blood flow per unit of time. Your spleen contracts, which releases more red blood cells into circulation. All non-essential processes – like digestion – slow down or stop.
>
> The high pressure of the gases has a narcotic effect. So in a very deep freedive – particularly on the ascent – you get into a woozy, almost drugged state, and you have to combat that and be present and concentrated.

Freediving is a sport that is practised in many forms across a variety of disciplines. From Static Apnea, where the diver stays perfectly still in the water and holds his or her breath for as long as possible (the world record at the time of writing is 22 minutes and 22 seconds held by Tom Sietas), to No-Limits Apnea, where the diver can descend and ascend using any equipment or method that he or she chooses (the current world record is 214 metres set by Herbert Nitsch), the sport encompasses a range of skill sets, technologies and physiologies. William Trubridge has made a name for himself in the sport by concentrating on two specific disciplines: Constant Weight Without Fins and Free Immersion. In the former category the diver descends and ascends without fins or the help of a rope – in essence he or she receives no assistance whatsoever in what is commonly termed the 'purest' form of freediving. In the Free Immersion category the diver can descend and ascend by pulling a rope, but again is not allowed any other assistance (from fins or mechanical equipment). Trubridge holds the world record in both categories – 101 metres in Constant Weight Without Fins and 121 metres in Free Immersion – and is the first and only person to swim below 100 metres in the Constant Weight Without Fins category.

Of course, Trubridge is constantly working on improving his physical strength to be able to dive deeper for longer. But the key to every successful dive – let alone record attempt – is an unwavering focus on managing his mental approach to the sport. As Trubridge himself admits, 'it's never something that you can completely master and it's a continual process'. His pre-dive preparation involves focusing his mind so that he is able to perform to his maximum ability.

> ❝ **I use visualisation** to prepare for every dive. I visualise every aspect of it and what I need to do and get right. That process is almost like a programming of your subconscious mind because you're telling it by images what you want it to achieve. You're programming that information in there so that during the dive itself your body and everything works without you having to make decisions or rationalise things or have any mental activity.

This is a constant process for Trubridge, and not just something that he engages in during a dive. Visualisation is one of the key parts of a varied training programme that sees the New Zealander training both his body and mind.

" **As I'm approaching** a record attempt I start adapting the body to high pressure and extreme depth and doing long dives. I have less volume of training in that period but I spend more time doing maximum attempts for dives. I also do a lot of exercises to increase the flexibility of my lungs, diaphragm and ribcage so that when I reach my target depth I am not going to injure myself or my lungs through what we call lung squeeze, which is where the pressure creates damage in your trachea or your lungs. In that period I also do mental preparation, visualisation and exercises to increase my confidence and programme my subconscious mind during the dive itself so that as much as possible I operate on autopilot.

During this training period – and, of course, in competition – when he has had a good dive Trubridge will use visualisation afterwards to 'embed' that dive into his subconscious, and so give himself a better chance of replicating it.

" **It helps to visualise** after a dive as it lets your mind feel like you've done a dive more than once.

This level of preparation helps Trubridge to relax ahead of a dive and execute that dive to the best of his abilities. It is a carefully managed process that is ongoing throughout the build-up to a dive – right up until the very last moments.

" **I will spend** at least 10 minutes lying on the dive platform with my eyes closed and lying on my back just concentrating on breathing naturally and relaxing. I am basically intending to fall asleep on the platform as this sort of stage is ideal for being able to freedive as you are completely relaxed. When I get into the water next to the dive line I continue lying on my back and breathing before starting the dive. That is maybe another five or

right Always focus on the positive execution of performance when visualising.

six minutes and still here trying to breathe naturally and not doing any special deep breathing. One of the main reasons behind that is obviously maintaining a healthy level of carbon dioxide. Then the last few breaths before the dive – the last two or three – is where I take longer, deeper breaths. And then the last breath itself I try and fill my lungs as much as possible.

Then William Trubridge dives.

We deal with some of the mind-management techniques Trubridge engages in the next chapter. However, visualisation prior to that dive plays a key role in preparing him for what he is about to do.

Visualisation is, of course, a very personal thing. It is also unique to every sport, and indeed the athlete's goals within that sport. As such, it is almost impossible to prescribe effective general techniques that enable athletes to visualise their performance. The simple fact that so many professional athletes from across the sporting spectrum call on this process to realise their goals is testament to the fact that it is an effective way of preparing the mind, and so the body, for a race or an event.

Amateur athletes do not always have to visualise every aspect of a race – and in endurance sports that is quite often impossible. However, an amateur athlete would undoubtedly benefit from using visualisation techniques when it comes to particularly difficult parts of an event – a tough climb on the bike or a difficult section of a run, for instance. This process of familiarisation and visualisation will undoubtedly help relax the mind, prepare the body and build an athlete's confidence ahead of an event.

above Visualisation is an effective tool to get you to the finish line of a race.

opposite Many pros visualise their performance all the way up to the beginning of a race.

VISUALISATION: KEY POINTS

- Visualisation can engage the senses of touch, taste, hearing and smell (not just vision).
- Begin with the basics: imagine yourself training in your favourite place.
- Always visualise positive actions. Focus on perfect technique or an ideal race outcome.
- Use it as a tool to train your subconscious mind to realise your goals.

9

Positivity:
Whether you think you can or you can't, you're right

Think of the thousands and thousands of thoughts that run through your head every day. Now think of the thousands that consume your mind about your sport and athletic performance. Now think of the words. When you talk to yourself (we all do it from time to time), what do you say? Are the majority of those thoughts and words positive or negative? For instance, when you think about the race that you are building up towards do you relish the opportunity to challenge yourself or do you dread the idea of tackling an event that is going to be a tough, physical grind? Do you tell yourself you can do it, or do you admit to yourself that it is going to be too hard? Hopefully – in both instances – it is the former. But if you go through the preparatory phase of your training and into the race itself believing and saying the latter, then the likelihood is that that will be your experience.

The way that you think about and perceive both your training sessions and the races that you enter will have a direct physical impact on your performance. If those thoughts and feelings are predominantly negative, then your body will respond accordingly. The same is true when those thoughts and feelings are positive. It makes sense when you think about it: when you are anxious or nervous your heart starts to race and your muscles tighten. Some athletes respond well to nerves and the tension that these invoke, but many fail to realise their aims and objectives because of the impact that nerves and anxiety have on them.

Negative *self-talk*

Psychologist Albert Ellis came up with a model to demonstrate how our thoughts and feelings impact our ability to realise our goals (it was not designed specifically with sports in mind, but can easily be employed in the sporting context). The premise of the model is A + B = C.

A = Activating event (for example: a race)

B = Belief (for example: it's going to be too hard)

C = Consequence (for example: anxiety, which leads to muscle tightness and underperformance)

William TRUBRIDGE

" It's never something that you can completely master and it's a continual process – you constantly have to keep in check the negative part of your mind which is throwing up worries or doubts. And you have to continually develop new techniques to give yourself confidence to relax or deal with that stress.

It is worth noting at this stage that the consequence is not the direct outcome of the subject's nervousness, rather the physical impact of the nervousness itself on the subject (in this instance, muscle tightness).

It is the physical impact of negativity on athletic performance that is one of the most important reasons why, as an athlete, it is important to take control over negative thoughts and negative self-talk. We will use the term 'negative self-talk' to encompass negative thoughts and the physical act of speaking to oneself as the effect is similar, if not the same.

When the individual adopts a negative attitude and engages in negative self-talk (with sayings such as: 'I can't do this', 'I will not achieve my goals' or 'I'm a failure') as Ellis succinctly encapsulated in A + B = C,

the effects on the overall feeling of the individual or athlete tends to range from worry/anxiety to despair/hopelessness. This in turn has a physiological effect (such as the tightening of the athlete's muscles), which will result in impaired performance.

If, however, an individual is able to counteract the negative self-talk with positive self-talk, the effect can be quite the opposite. Phrases like 'I can do this' will help to motivate an athlete, engendering a sense of positive purpose. What's more, this positivity will help an athlete to relax. By relaxation, we mean channelling energy and adrenalin into positive motivation in preparation for performance (not the 'sit in a comfortable sofa and think happy thoughts' kind of relaxation). In so doing, an athlete is preparing his or her body to realise their maximum capabilities.

This is easier said than done. Many human beings are hard-wired to be negative. It's not a deliberate thing, it is a simple fact of life. What's more, in the specific case of endurance events – which are designed to be tough – the likelihood of doubt or negativity creeping into the psyche of an athlete is higher than in a lot of conventional sports (although the impacts can be just as profound regardless of the pursuit). As a result, learning to deal with these thoughts as they arise – both before, during and after performance – is an essential skill set for endurance athletes to master.

To do this well, though, it is important to adopt a holistic approach to dealing with negative self-talk. It is no good simply adopting a positive approach to sport if the rest of your life is overwhelmingly dominated by negative thoughts. In this instance, it is likely that the negativity will eventually override the positivity when the mind and body are fatigued. Consequently, it is important that you try to address negative self-talk across every aspect of your life, from work to social interactions to sport. It is also important to realise that these thoughts manifest themselves in a variety of guises, from taking things too personally to being a complete perfectionist (as in all areas of life, nobody in sport can get everything right every time) to blaming other people for your shortcomings. You should try and monitor your thought processes and catch the negative thoughts as they appear.

below Solo sports like round the world sailing place enormous demands on an athlete's mind.

Once you have 'caught' them, though, what should you do with them? There are many techniques employed by sports psychologists for dealing with negative self-talk and their success depends on the motivating factors of the individual. Some sports psychologists recommend strategies like carrying a rubber band around your wrist and flicking yourself with it every time a negative thought enters your head. Other techniques involve simply accepting the thought into the mind and letting it 'wash through'. In this respect, you do not fight the negative thought, but almost welcome it, reducing the fear or nervousness that the thought can engender (this is a technique commonly adopted by freedivers).

However, in the context of prolonged physical activity like endurance sports there may be drawbacks to both of the above approaches (although if you find that they work for you, then fantastic!). In the specific instance of endurance sports it is more be beneficial to adopt a strategy of affirmation throughout all aspects of your life, and back that strategy up with techniques for countering these thoughts. Below are some of these techniques.

SELF-AFFIRMATION

The majority of endurance athletes go into an event knowing what to expect. Even if they have never done a particular distance before, they have a basic understanding of the demands that the sport – and the distance – will place on their bodies. As a result, they plan and train accordingly. This is where self-affirmation becomes invaluable. Once you have developed a training plan and started to execute on that plan, it is beneficial to remind yourself of the reasons why you are tackling these sessions and how your performance has improved as a result of them. For instance, thinking 'This six-hour ride is going to make me stronger on race day' or 'I am running faster than I've ever run before' or 'I can feel my swim improving with every length of the pool'. Of course, sometimes it can be counter-intuitive to do this. Those are the times when self-affirmation is most important. By teaching the brain to take an overwhelmingly positive approach to your training, you will start to reap the physical rewards of this mentality.

COUNTERING THE THOUGHT

If you start with the premise that endurance sports are mentally and physically tough and take place over an extended period of time, it is easy to see why negative thoughts can be a factor for many athletes. When those thoughts arise, you have the choice between either accepting the thought and the resulting impact that it will have on your performance, or making a mental effort to counter that thought. When a thought like 'I'm not strong enough to finish this race' creeps into your mind, the response needs to be quick and immediate: 'I have trained for this and I am strong enough to do this.' In essence, you are taking a logical stance against an illogical thought pattern borne from physical and mental fatigue.

RESTRUCTURE A THOUGHT

Endurance races are hard and most athletes who have competed one can remember times when the sheer physicality of what they were doing was nigh on overwhelming. In these instances, it can be tempting to think: 'I can't do this, I'm out of energy.' If the mind believes that, the body will respond. However, it is perfectly feasible to restructure that thought to say: 'I'm tired and I need to refuel and rehydrate. I'm going to take a minute to do that and then I am going to be back on track.' Restructuring a thought is simply a question of taking a more positive approach to a negative thought pattern, and it can produce immediate results.

---

right When negative thoughts creep into your mind try to counter or restructure them.

Managing negative **self-talk**

Like many of the psychological approaches examined in this book, managing negative self-talk takes time and focus. Athletes who are able to do it and who can subsequently adopt a more positive approach to their sport – and hopefully their lives as a whole – will see a vastly improved level of performance. As Albert Ellis's ABC model indicated, the body responds directly to the thoughts and feelings of the mind, and a positive mind will drive a positive body. In short, as legendary car manufacturer and industrialist Henry Ford once famously said (from which this chapter takes its title): 'Whether you think you can or you can't, you're right.'

In Chapter 8 (Visualisation: Seeing is believing) we discussed William Trubridge's use of visualisation as a means of preparing his mind for a record-breaking dive.

However, once underwater Trubridge has to try to close off the mind from thoughts entirely.

> " **During the dive** itself I try as much as possible not to have any thoughts as thoughts themselves are brainwaves which take energy and oxygen to create. If you can limit that then you can reduce your oxygen consumption. Obviously that's one of the hardest things to do in any circumstance, let alone when you are stressing out about something.

The nature of freediving means that Trubridge's approach to dealing with negative thoughts is relatively unique in the endurance sports context.

> " **If a negative** thought comes into my head and I try to push it out or not think about it then often that creates a condition where it gets worse. So rather than trying to actively oppose it I concentrate on the spaces between the thoughts. There's no way to describe the process but I'm basically trying to lengthen the space between the thoughts and enjoy those rather than focusing on the thoughts themselves. So I let the thoughts just slide in and slide out, and eventually they become more and more scarce and your mind slows down.

As discussed in Chapter 8 (Visualisation: Seeing is believing) there are various physiological reasons behind the slowing down of the mind. However, regardless of the physiology or the means that he uses to manage those thoughts, there are few sports where being in control of the mind is as essential as it is in freediving. In some instances it can be a matter of life or death. As a result, Trubridge is constantly battling with a mind that looks to allow negativity to creep in.

> " **It's never something** that you can completely master and it's a continual process – you constantly have to keep in check the negative part of your mind which is throwing up worries or doubts. And you have

right The freediver tries to slow the mind right down.

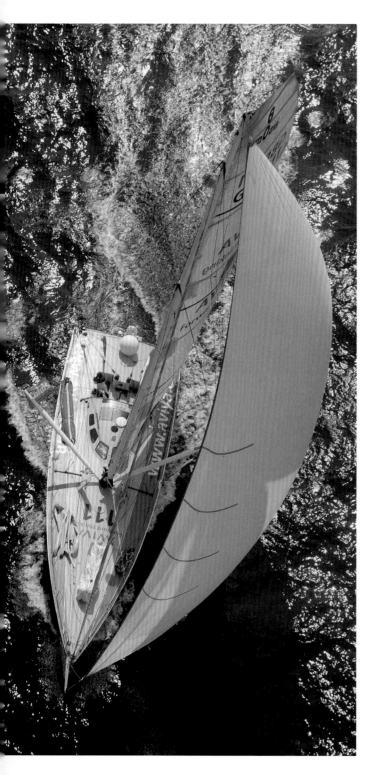

to continually develop new techniques to give yourself confidence to relax or deal with that stress. As you use techniques they get old and stop working after a while so you have to continually stay one step ahead of your mind and your subconscious in order to be able to master it.

To achieve what he has achieved, William Trubridge has had to develop effective ways of dealing with negativity. And while freediving is relatively extreme in terms of the level at which athletes are required to manage their minds and thought processes, the basic premise rings true for athletes across the sporting spectrum.

Banishing **negativity**
DEE CAFFARI

Managing negative self-talk is certainly something record-breaking yachtswoman Dee Caffari discovered that she needed to do during her first solo circumnavigation of the globe.

The Southern Ocean is a formidable foe. Located between 60 degrees south latitude and the South Pole, it is a huge circumpolar body of water. Unique among the oceans, it has no landmass to its north and the current always travels eastwards. What's more, the change in temperature between air of the Antarctic ice and the air on the open ocean helps to whip up cyclonic winds (which also head eastwards) that have little, if anything, to impede their journey. Because of this, the Southern Ocean boasts the strongest average wind speeds found anywhere on Earth.

It was against this backdrop – and the currents and winds of the Southern Ocean – that Dee Caffari cemented her name in sailing's history books. In 2005 Caffari set off on a solo, single-handed voyage around the world. That alone is a feat. But unlike any other woman

left The Southern Ocean is a lonely place.

in history, Caffari was sailing westwards against the wind and prevailing currents of the Southern Ocean. She returned 178 days later to a hero's welcome. For Caffari, quite understandably, it was an eye-opening experience.

❝ **It's extreme** – extreme on every front. The temperatures are so cold because of the wind chill and the icy water. So your fingers are frozen within seconds of being on deck. The walls of water have so much power behind them that it's incredible; you have no control over it and there's no easy get-out.

Everything is loaded massively so if anything does go wrong then it goes wrong in a massive way: you're on the edge of control. But these conditions are what the boat is designed for. I remember the first thought when I was in the Southern Ocean was 'how do I slow this boat down?' It took me a while – about ten days – to learn that I don't slow the boat down, it's what it's designed to do, and actually the faster you go the better it is. So it's a massive mental game and physically it's demanding because the conditions are so difficult. But that's the buzz, that's why we go down there.

It was that buzz that attracted Caffari back to the Southern Ocean just two years after completing her first circumnavigation. In 2008 she took part in a race that is widely heralded as being the Everest of sailing: the Vendée Globe.

❝ **For me to be** the first woman to go the 'wrong' way round was quite unique, but I was very aware as I crashed through the Southern Ocean that everybody else goes the other way. So I decided that I wanted to find out why they go that way – it seemed much easier in comparison. And if you're going to put yourself out there to do that then the ultimate way to do it is with the best sailors in the world in the pinnacle event, which is the Vendée Globe.

On the surface, the Vendée Globe might seem to be easier – Caffari completed the race in little over 99 days – but the challenges involved were different for Caffari.

❝ **When I set off** the wrong way round it was about adventure and being the first woman to do something – I took an opportunity that presented itself. It was about completing it and I learnt a lot along the way. But my sailing has evolved and I'm in a competitive arena and now it is about performance. I've ticked the boxes, I've got some world records and I've delivered. But now I've upped my game and want to put myself where the big boys are.

Trans-oceanic sailing is a punishing, and at times dangerous, pursuit. To be successful – and fast – a sailor has to take calculated risks and push both themselves and their boats to the limits of what they are capable of.

❝ **As I'm developing** and getting more competitive I'm spending a bit more time on the edge of control, which is where I'm meant to be if I'm going to be pushing hard and making the boat go faster. So at times you deal with it all and then you realise that actually what you've done was quite scary, but you don't think about how scary it is before you do it.

You know what the task is and you focus fully on that and you're so involved in this boat and performance and positions and the race that your outside thoughts of 'actually I'm thousands of miles from rescue and things are quite scary', you can't actually think about it. It's a bit like crossing the road and being scared that you might get run over by a bus. You'd never go out if you had that thought in the forefront of your mind the whole time. It's just about having that focus and being determined to see something through to the end.

Managing the variables that Caffari faced while out at sea was far from easy. Not only is there a significant element of danger when it comes to tackling some of the world's most ferocious seas, but hers is a lonely pursuit. Of course, during an expedition or race Caffari maintains regular contact with her team, but those interactions tend to be more functional than friendly, meaning that for all intents and purposes she is alone. That solitude, coupled with the need to manage the mind under extreme levels of emotional and physical stress, was something that Caffari had to learn to deal with during her first circumnavigation.

❝ **When I went** the wrong way around the world I just took it on and thought I'd learn about it on the way round. It was my first solo experience and one of the hardest things to deal with was spending 24 hours a day with myself – that was the biggest shock to the system. I spent a lot of time on this exhausting emotional roller coaster: one minute I was happy and smiley, the next in tears.

Caffari was struggling to manage her mind. Of course, that is completely understandable given not only the nature of the challenge, but the impossibility of

preparing for the rigours of that challenge in advance. However, if her first circumnavigation of the globe – ironically the toughest of her three circumnavigations – was a learning exercise, her second was a serious race. And in a bid to raise her level to that of the best in the world Caffari realised that she had to 'cross all of the Ts and dot all of the Is'.

Of course, physical and boat preparation demanded the majority of her time. However, as part of her development she also sought help managing her mental state while out at sea.

❝ **I worked with** a sports psychologist and he asked me to keep a record. Every time I went offshore – training or doing a shorter race – I kept a log of what activity I did, what food I ate, when I slept and how I

below Dee Caffari.

was feeling each day. It was quite detailed and it was a big commitment but the benefits were huge.

This work continued throughout the duration of the Vendée Globe. As part of a study conducted by Dr Neil Weston at the University of Plymouth, Caffari filled out a spread sheet every day detailing her nutrition, hydration, sleep and mood (among other things). This allowed Dr Weston to track her mental state throughout the race, determining the peaks and troughs in her emotions and how they matched up to variables such as sleep and nutrition. When Caffari returned from the Vendée Globe, she met with Dr Weston to discuss the findings from this study.

> *I was diagnosed* – it sounds as if I was seeing a shrink – that my default setting was very negative. I could always tell people what I didn't want to happen but I didn't have the confidence to tell people what I did want to happen.

I didn't want to let my team down, I didn't want to be last, I didn't want to be the last girl, I didn't want to be slow. But I wasn't prepared to say 'Okay, I want to keep my boat going above 10 knots' or 'I want to keep pushing to that weather system'. I couldn't take it to positive things.

Rather than always erring on the side of caution, or telling people what I didn't want to happen, I had to physically change that so I was consciously thinking about pushing and boat speed and performance. I was constantly realigning my thoughts.

In many ways, Caffari was learning about the importance of controlling the controllables (as we discuss in Chapter 6). But by developing techniques

below As well as two solo circumnavigations, Dee Caffari has sailed round the world as part of a team.

to manage her negativity, she was also learning the importance of communicating effectively with her team to allow them to give her maximum support and assistance. Races like the Vendée Globe are defined in the media as solo efforts. And while it is true that it is one sailor against the mighty ocean, behind that sailor is a team working tirelessly to give her or him the information that they need to successfully complete a race. In Caffari's case, that included a boat project manager to oversee technical aspects of boat maintenance, and an overall project manager, who also happened to be her partner.

Following the completion of Dr Weston's study, Caffari was able to reassess how she communicated with her crew to produce the most effective results.

> ❝ **I learnt very quickly** that I needed to concentrate on the things I could do something about and not stress about the things I could do nothing about. I needed to have the right conversation with my shore team so that was invaluable to tell them what information I didn't want to have.

The process of assessing her personality wasn't easy for Caffari. However, having opened herself up for analysis and taken on board the results, she has found that it has had a significant impact on her life.

> ❝ **Now I can go** sailing and instead of all of this emotional energy being wasted I can actually push that into the performance side of the boat because I can do something about that. I can't do something about the weather or how fast someone else's boat is going, I'm now much more streamlined. It's also helped me in my day-to-day living; I'm much more realistic and it's helped me prioritise goals a little easier and – most of the time – I've reduced my stress levels.

The process of changing the 'default setting' of an individual's personality takes time and constant work. Even now, Caffari has to work to maintain a positive attitude.

> ❝ **Every now and again** I slip into that default setting and I have to have a word with myself.

Caffari has seen first-hand the benefits of adopting a positive mindset, and the importance of positive self-talk. She has also witnessed the impact of negative self-talk while out at sea. While the negativity during her first solo circumnavigation of the globe can be attributed to factors such as sleep deprivation and lack of nutrition, a fundamental part of that attitude was down to personality traits. Recognising those traits and working to change them has had a huge impact, not only on her ability as a sailor but on her general attitude to life.

The human mind is as fragile as it is strong. What we as individuals believe or tell ourselves has a huge impact on how our bodies perform. If our beliefs are overwhelmingly negative, the body will respond as such. The same is true if the mind is overwhelmingly positive. As such, it stands to reason that for an athlete to perform at their best they need to believe in their own abilities. A solid training base can help develop that belief, but needs to be backed up by a positive mental attitude. When combined, the two make for a formidable combination.

POSITIVITY: KEY POINTS

- The way you think and feel about a training session or race will directly influence your performance.
- Positivity is holistic: it needs to be practised both in and away from the sporting arena.
- Use techniques such as self-affirmation and restructuring a thought to counter negativity.
- Focus on the things that you want and need, not the things that you don't want and don't need.

10

Adaptation:
Improvise to overcome

Every athlete goes into a race with a strategy. That strategy might be as simple as going slow and steady while managing nutrition and hydration on the way to hitting an overall target time. But it might also be more complex, and involve pacing particular phases of a race while responding to the tactics of an opponent. Whatever strategy the athlete adopts, it should always carry one key element: it has to be flexible.

As we discussed in Chapter 6 (Control: The management of the self), an essential element of both the preparation and execution of a race-day strategy is the ability to control the controllables. In this respect, you can control your strategy and the management of your nutrition and hydration (as long as nothing goes wrong). However, such is the nature of any given race day that there are numerous variables outside of your control that can – and will – have a direct impact on your performance. These variables can be anything from the weather to the actions of an opponent or the performance of your equipment on the day. How you respond to those variables and adapt your strategy to them will very often determine the outcome of your race.

Brett Sutton has forged a considerable reputation for himself by coaching some of the biggest names in both the short- and long-course triathlon. And while he is famous for implementing a tough training regimen with his athletes, his approach to race-day strategy focuses on improving mental strength as well as physical ability.

> ❝ **You've got mind sports** like tennis and golf, where the mental aspect of the sport overtakes the physical. They are sports where you have to play the big points well. A lot of the other sports you have to be physically extremely precocious, train and have a different mindset to win. I put Ironman in that category of the mind sports because you have to control yourself for eight hours – you can't go flat out the whole time. It's basically a thinking man's sport.

For Sutton, success in long-distance triathlon is dependent on the athlete's ability to manage the body. As such, his athletes are taught to adjust – and readjust if necessary – their race plans to give themselves the best possible chance of success.

Rendy Lynn **OPDYCKE**

> ❝ You know that you're opening Pandora's Box on race day, so you need to always be comfortable with a changing dynamic situation.

above Before any race you should prepare for as many eventualities as possible.

❛❛ **Ironman is about** making the right decisions at the right time. Very few athletes can do that. You get the real good ones who can back off when they have to back off and who can take an extra two minutes for their feeding strategy because something has gone wrong. Whereas the other guys press on and think they can get an extra few minutes down the road and work it out. It's the ability to not panic when things go wrong.

Sutton's path into triathlon was unconventional, to say the least. Coming from a family of coaches, the Australian started to teach swimming at the age of ten and had his own squad by the time he was 15. However, many parents struggled with the idea of a teenager teaching their children to swim, and so Sutton turned his attention to animals; namely horses and greyhounds. A precocious character, he took up squash and boxing – becoming an Australian champion in the latter – before moving back into swimming and then to triathlon. His experience across this broad range of sports has had a huge impact on his approach to coaching athletes.

❛❛ **In Ironman** there is no race where you are not going to have a situation where you have to be defensive. People laugh at me because I do so much of my talking about triathlon in and around boxing, which I'm intimately involved with and know a lot about. If you're a great fighter and don't know how to defend in boxing you don't last very long. Triathletes think defence is something that you put around a house. In golf everyone can hit a 66, but it's the guys who on a bad day can pull out the club and say 'On a good day I can hit this seven-iron right to the heart of the green but I'm not playing that well today so I'm going to play a different stroke because I'm not really on it.' That mentality is much more in tune with triathlon than nearly everyone gives it credit for.

Triathletes have to have that ability to compromise and overcome different situations. That's how I read it, and that's where I differ from a lot of other people. A lot of people think I'm 'ra ra ra' but of the people who know me only one in ten will see me standing at the side of an Ironman saying 'go harder, go harder' – that's total bullshit. If you're in an Ironman then the likelihood is that you're doing the best you can. You need to have your ability about you, know your pacing and know what you're doing.

So I'm different from a lot of people – I don't really believe that a triathlon is a race until you get down to the last 12 kilometres. The rest of it is monitoring

below Triathletes must have the ability to compromise and overcome difficult situations.

yourself and making sure you can hit the numbers you are capable of.

Daniel Halksworth's first Ironman win at the 2012 Ironman UK is a perfect example of the implementation of his coach's approach to racing. Halksworth, who had been part of Brett Sutton's teamTBB squad for two years, entered the second transition alongside 2010 Ironman UK champion Fraser Cartmell. Having raced the majority of the bike within touching distance of one another, out on the run the two athletes' strategies differed dramatically. Cartmell set off hard, opening up a lead of more than a minute over the first six miles, while Halksworth bided his time. He managed his nutrition and hydration and stopped briefly for a toilet break. As Sutton would have predicted, slowly Cartmell started to fall back. Six miles further down the road – by the mid-point of the race – Cartmell and Halksworth were running side by side, and at the end of the marathon Halksworth was nearly 12 minutes up on his rival. Of course, it is difficult not to factor in the individual circumstances of the race, but as Halksworth later stated:

❝ **Brett said go out there** and run your race and make sure you don't push it at the start. It's a long race and if someone is in front of you and they are going

well things can change after 20 kilometres. He's pushed those things into my head and it seems to be working.

Sutton's approach is rigorous. Athletes are expected to do exactly what they are told to do at all times, whether or not they want to do it. That does not necessarily mean always working them hard, although he is famous for his gruelling training regimens. But as Nicola Spirig's win at the London 2012 Olympics shows (detailed in Chapter 14 – When it all comes together) there is a methodology behind this approach. By pushing his athletes above and beyond what they feel they are capable of doing in training, Sutton helps to instil in them a confidence that they take through to race day. That confidence gives his

athletes the freedom to adapt their strategies and realise a positive outcome even in adverse conditions.

❝ **If you're a boxer** you know within 50 seconds of the first round if today physically you feel wrecked. You don't think every boxer turns up and by the end of round two they're feeling fantastic. Some guys physically are awful. In triathlon, people then turn off and say 'I get aches because I'm having a bad day.' When you're a boxer you're looking across the ring at somebody who has a legal licence to kill you. At that point it's not 'I'm having a bad day', it's about 'how do I overcome my bad day'. That's why I use that for Ironman. Not because there's anything remotely similar with the sports, but because of the mentality. The mentality is very, very similar.

You have to improvise, overcome, know yourself, know when you need to back off, know when you need to attack. For me, I think psychologically I get much closer to my athletes because I have been a professional fighter. Everyone else is walking around saying 'How can he do that? It's got nothing to do with it.' It's got everything to do with mentality.

Sutton's attitude towards racing might be tough, but he has proven time and time again that it works. And not just with pro triathletes. Sutton cites one of his greatest achievements as a coach as helping one athlete take four hours off her Ironman time so that she could finish a race in sub-10 hours. While physical conditioning is undoubtedly the driving force behind this improvement in levels of performance, adapting the athlete's mental approach to their sport is similarly important. Numerous athletes coached by Sutton refer to the emphasis that the Australian places on adaptation and flexibility in a racing strategy, and it is the athlete's confidence and ability to respond to the changing nature of a race that sees so many of them scoring wins at their target events.

left A boxer has to adapt to the changing nature of a fight. Successful endurance athletes learn to do the same.

Know your *As + Bs + Cs*

RENDY LYNN OPDYCKE

Every athlete experiences days when the body or the mind isn't quite as tuned in to performing as the individual would hope. In those instances it is up to the athlete to decide whether to adapt accordingly and push through to realise a strong performance, or to succumb to temptation to write a race off as a 'bad day'.

In some sports, variables outside of the control of the athlete can determine how good or bad the race day will be. Open water swimming is a challenging pursuit that pits an athlete against their bodies, minds, and more variables that are out of their control than most other sports. In some controlled races – such as the 10km marathon swim raced at the Olympics – athletes complete multiple loops of courses in still bodies of open water. For the most part, however, the majority of open water swim meets take place in active bodies of water where tides, currents and waves pose a very real obstacle to completion. The races vary in length from a couple of kilometres to what is the longest organised open water swimming race in the world: the 88km Maraton Acuatico Internacional Hernandarias-Paraná in Argentina. Of course, athletes attempt longer challenges, and various bids are made to cross significant bodies of water or circumnavigate islands year after year.

Regardless of the race – or the challenge the athlete sets him or herself – the rigours of the sport remain the same. Open water swimmers can boast a mental and physical strength that many athletes only aspire towards, and they can adapt themselves to cope with the numerous variables that are thrown at them during an event.

Rendy Lynn Opdycke has carved a formidable reputation for herself in open water swimming circles. Opdycke has been swimming almost since the day she was born. The American was small at birth (4lbs, 6oz) and doctors told her parents to 'swim' her in a bath to get her muscles going. So began a love affair

above Different stages of different races can throw up multiple scenarios.

with the water that would see her attempt a perilous open water solo swim to and from an island one mile away aged eight (she was grounded after being picked up by lifeguards) and culminated in a record-breaking completion of the Triple Crown of Swimming.

To be recognised for completing the Triple Crown an athlete must swim the English Channel (approximately 22 miles/35 kilometres, though the exact distance depends on the tide), the Manhattan Island Marathon Swim (28.5 miles/45.8 kilometres), and the Santa

Catalina Channel in California (22 miles/35 kilometres). In 2008 Opdycke completed all three swims within 35 days (5 July to 9 August), the shortest time in the history of the Triple Crown. What's more, her cumulative time of 27 hours and 9 minutes was – at that time – the fastest that anyone had completed all three challenges.

Rules and regulations around these swims are tight. The swimmer is allowed no artificial aids and may only wear a standard swimming costume, goggles, swim cap, nose clip and ear plugs. They may grease the body for warmth. In the case of Channel crossings, the swimmer must start on dry land and finish on 'the opposite coast with no seawater beyond' them. Finally, they are allowed no physical contact with either the boat or the people on it.

Needless to say, over long periods of time and the inevitably changing conditions through these active bodies of water it is essential that the swimmer is able to adapt to manage their progress. During the course of her short, but impressively successful, swim career Opdycke has become a master of doing just that.

❝ *I have my plans:* A, B and C. Plan A is Plan A but the plans have to be pretty fluid because it's Mother Nature, and you never really know what you're going to get. She often changes her plans by the minute so even though the weatherman says there's high probability of 'what-not', other things can always happen. You always have to know that you're playing in her terrain and you have to play her game. Plan B is obviously a little more fluid than Plan A. And Plan C … Plan C is sometimes when it's the determining factor of whether you're going to finish or not. It's out of your hands and it's the boat crew or the coaches who have to make the call.

I have had Plan C come about when I was on a relay and we were trying to become the first relay to swim from Santa Rosa to the mainland. Unfortunately, a situation came up where we thought we might have to quit the race because the swells were more than seven feet and it was getting dark and we knew the currents would change. That's when you have to think about calling off the swim – and that becomes a collective decision.

Fortunately, during her record-breaking Triple Crown bid Opdycke was able to juggle the demands of the three formidable bodies of water relying on Plan A and, occasionally, Plan B. The latter was called on during the course of her English Channel crossing – the second, and for Opdycke the most challenging of the three legs of the Crown.

❝ *I think the* English Channel was the most difficult leg because it's not in my backyard and I had to travel there. So there were the unknowns of getting all my stuff together and my crew together; the difference in the salinity content of the water there – it's much more salty; the unknown factor of it all. Also, it's the fact that it's the English Channel. It's the Channel we all associate with difficulty. It is the crème de la crème of open water swimming, and everyone knows about it. So it's got an ominous feeling to it.

On the day of her crossing, Opdycke had every reason to feel nervous. Over the course of the swim winds whipped up the body of water, with a six-foot swell running through the Channel, leaving the American battling a churning sea of icy cold water.

❝ *There were times* when I knew that I needed to change it up; when I started to have self-doubt. About halfway through the temperature changed to about five degrees cooler and I had to start thinking about tropical islands and warm places and singing songs that were related to heat factors. I had to mentally change the aspect of my thinking so I wouldn't think about the cold weather and the fact that I was cold.

What's more, nearing the conclusion of the race she had to respond to the demands of her team to increase her pace when the currents started to change.

❝ *I was physically* feeling like I was going hard but I had David Clark with me – a famous swimmer and the one that encouraged me to do distance swimming – when I was in the Channel and he was like 'you've got to push it pretty hard' because the currents were

above When you play with Mother Nature you never really know what you're going to get.

switching and pulling me. At this point near the finish of the crossing if I could not have picked up the pace I would have missed the lighthouse on the shore. If you miss that marker point you're going to be swimming for an additional amount of time and distance. This is the breaking point for most swimmers' attempts due to the current change, the duration spent in the water and the sheer physical exhaustion. If the swimmer is unable to dig deep and muster up an additional effort then they might not finish.

The English Channel is notoriously tough because of three main factors: the cold, the traffic (it is one of the busiest shipping lanes in the world) and the tides that push through it. Swimmers only attempt to cross the Channel at optimum times, and even then they end up swimming in an 'Z' across the body of water as the tide pushes them to and fro. Opdycke was able to respond to Clark's calls and successfully completed the English Channel crossing in 10 hours and 54 minutes en route to her place in the record books.

Repeatedly, though, Opdycke can reference scenarios where she's had to change her strategy and plans because of the changing demands of a race. Before sealing the Triple Crown Opdycke did something that few other women in open water swimming competitions have managed to do: win a major international swimming race outright. On 24 June 2006 the American took to the waters off Manhattan's Battery Park and began her second attempt at the 28.5 mile Manhattan Island Marathon Swim. In 2004 she had finished second overall (first woman), but in 2006 she won the event outright in a time of 7 hours, 27 minutes and 26 seconds. She was more than 22 minutes ahead of the second-placed man – the largest margin of victory in the history of the race.

The race was run under difficult conditions, with swimmers briefly pulled from the water as a lightning storm lashed Manhattan Island.

> **Manhattan is always** one that is a challenge because of the time and the date that they do the race. They have a lot of white squall come in and twice out of the four times I have done it they have had points when they have to pull the swimmers out. And that's difficult because if you get pulled out and then, after a period of time, they tell you to get back in you physically stop working and your muscles have a bunch of lactic acid in them and they're stiff, and it's very difficult to mentally get back into race mode.

The nature of open water swimming – like many endurance events – dictates that athletes have to accept and adapt to the changing face of a race. Occasionally personal circumstances call on the swimmer to change tactics or levels of effort, but often it is conditions beyond their control that force them to do so. Like most successful athletes, Rendy Lynn Opdycke has achieved her goals because she has developed an approach to racing that allows her to adapt her strategy. This ability to adapt is essential, because as Opdycke herself reflects:

> **You know that** you're opening Pandora's Box on race day, so you need to always be comfortable with a changing dynamic situation.

below 'You're opening Pandora's Box on race day' – Rendy Lynn Opdyke

Putting it all on the *line*
STEPHEN ROCHE

Few sports combine tactical awareness and intense physicality like road cycling. At the pinnacle of the sport, Grand Tours take place over multiple weeks, and cyclists are constantly developing and adapting their tactics to adjust to counter-attacks by rival teams on stages that vary dramatically day by day. These days, cyclists and their teams have plenty of technology at their disposal. Teams are linked via radios, with team cars monitoring the action and making strategy decisions as each stage in the race unfolds. This constant communication not only helps to shape the race, but also allows individual riders to manage their levels of effort as teams dictate the roles of the riders during the course of a stage.

Of course, it hasn't always been like this. In fact, regular radio communication between the cyclists and the Tour 'caravan' is a relatively recent evolution – the Motorola team of the 1990s are believed to have pioneered the practice – and it only became commonplace in 2002. Before that, cyclists had to rely on the imprecise timings of strategically placed watchers on the road, not to mention their own wits and cunning. In short, they had to watch and adapt as the race unfolded around them.

It was against this backdrop that in 1987 Stephen Roche realised the pinnacle of his career: winning the Triple Crown of road cycling. By winning the Giro d'Italia, Tour de France and World Road Cycling Championships in one year, Roche became only the second man in the history of the sport to achieve this feat (the first was Eddy Merckx in 1974).

The manner in which Roche realised his goals was impressive. On Stage 15 of the Giro d'Italia Roche attacked the leader of the race, his Italian teammate Roberto Visentini. The attack came from a long way out and despite the team working for Visentini – against Roche – they were unable to bridge the gap to the Irishman. Much to the ire of his team and the Italian

above The most famous finish line in world cycling.

crowd, Roche wore the Maglia Rosa for the remainder of the Giro, claiming a historic win as the first man from outside of mainland Europe to take the title.

In typical style, Roche refused to savour his victory and instead drove straight to Paris to prepare for the Tour. With reigning champion Greg LeMond ruled out following a shooting accident, Roche started to plan for the 25-stage, 4,231km race (the last truly 'long' Tour – thereafter the races were shorter and competed over 21, and then 23 days).

> ❝ *I looked at* the guys around me who I thought I would be competing with at the end. And the main men would be Jean-François Bernard, Charly Mottet, Pedro Delgado – I analysed them all and I marked their boxes.

This analysis was an ongoing process, and Roche's race strategy changed according to who was performing and who wasn't.

> ❝ *After ten days* of racing I said 'Okay, my main man is Delgado, what am I going to have to do to beat him? I have ten days coming, I've got a lot of climbing, I've not got a good climbing team, I'm a good climber myself but I'm not a climber like Delgado, so how am I going to do this?' So I dictated my own strategy. That

strategy was 'Okay, the final time trial is in Dijon so if I can be within one minute of Delgado I'm still capable of winning the Tour because I reckon that in 45 kilometres if it came down to it I could put a minute into Delgado. So if I'm within a minute of Delgado going into the final time trial I can still win the Tour. If I'm a minute and a half it's very dodgy – it's going to be very difficult to beat Delgado.' In actual fact – just to show you how well I knew myself – I put 61 seconds into Delgado in the final time trial. That's the way I planned my last ten days in the mountains and the other stages.

On the surface, the plan sounded simple. In reality, Roche rode himself into unconsciousness – and Tour folklore – on the 185km stage between Le Bourg-d'Oisans and La Plagne. Having attacked early on the stage, Roche was caught by the General Classification (GC) leader Pedro Delgado some 40 kilometres from the mountaintop finish line. Delgado pushed on, leaving Roche in his wake. At the last official time check going onto the mountain the Spaniard was well over a minute ahead of the Irishman – having taken a 25-second GC advantage into the stage – and with the days of the Tour running out, Roche knew that Stage 21 was make or break for his title chances.

❝ **I had attacked** Delgado from very far out. He caught me on the final climb and I knew if I tried to stay with him he'd kill me because he was a much stronger climber than me. So I thought that I'd let him go, let him think that he was winning and I would try to recuperate and see what happens.

I realised quickly that I could hold him at a minute – a minute and a half. So was I holding him at a minute and a half because he was holding back, or was he wasted? Was he going as fast as he could? When I realised that he wasn't taking any more time out of me I thought: 'I'll hold him now at 1:10, 1:15, 1:20', he thinks he's winning it and then in the final 4 kilometres I'll give it everything I have to try and get back as close as I can to him – and hopefully get back to within 30 seconds of him and keep my Tour options open.

With 4 kilometres to go I gave it everything. Because there were no radios – which was a good thing at the time – I gave it everything I had and, to my great surprise and to everyone else's, I came back to within four seconds of him. But I basically had to bury myself. I had to get back into my window of one minute. I was 1:20 down with 4 kilometres to go, plus the 25 seconds I was in arrears starting the stage, so my Tour chances were getting slimmer. With 4 kilometres to go I gave it everything and I got to within four seconds of the guy and that left my Tour options open.

Despite intense pressure and fatigue accumulated during the Tour de France, Roche made the decision to adjust his race strategy to suit the reality of the competition. The coverage of those final minutes of Stage 21 of the 1987 Tour de France is legendary. Following an all-out dash to the line Roche collapsed, with medics administering oxygen for 30 minutes before the Irishman was truly able to savour his victory. To further cement his place in Tour folklore, the first words Roche are reported to have said following his recovery were: 'Everything's okay, *mais pas de femme ce soir*.' [No woman for me tonight.]

Not many athletes would be able to bury themselves in such emphatic style. But as we see in Chapter 13 (Winning: it's all in the mind) Roche was motivated purely by the thought of winning the Tour de France above all other considerations.

❝ **How often** do you get a chance to win the Tour de France? I'm in there still with a chance to win it and what do I do? Do I let it go? Do I leave it for next year or do I give it a go? I didn't purposefully put myself into a semi-coma. I did my best just to get as close as I could to Delgado.

You just look at the road in front of you. There's no point in listening to time checks – well you can, but with all the shouting that was going on at the side of the road you don't know whether they are reliable time checks or not. So you just bury yourself. If I had known that Delgado was only 30 seconds ahead of me

above Stephen Roche rode himself into unconsciousness in pursuit of victory.

I probably would have backed off. I would have backed off and thought 'I'm within a minute.' I would have been content with 30 seconds. I knew that once he crossed the finishing line his stopwatch stopped and I would have to get those seconds back somewhere. So I basically had to just keep going.

History records that Frenchman Laurent Fignon won Stage 21 of the 1987 Tour de France. However, on that day Stephen Roche arguably won the greatest cycle race on Earth. He did that the only way he knew how: by giving everything in the pursuit of victory. However, his win involved more than simply giving every ounce of energy that he possessed. Rather, it was a tactical victory. And it was one that epitomised the importance of adapting to situations as they unfold, not only on

the day but throughout the duration of a race. Roche monitored his competition, determined the pace he felt able to sustain, and attacked when he knew he had the best possible chance of succeeding. These tactics were determined by the Irishman alone, and were managed while the race unfolded around him. It was a masterful execution of a racing strategy, and it won Stephen Roche the biggest prize in his sport.

Athletes have to be able to adapt. There are simply too many variables at play on a race day not to do so. Whether that adaptation is a result of the tactics and movements of an opponent, the whims of Mother Nature, or because the body and mind do not feel like performing on a given day, the truth of the matter is that to realise pre-race goals – whether that be to hit a target time or to win the Tour de France – an athlete has to mould their strategy around their race.

Of course, adapting a race-day strategy calls on many elements we discuss throughout this book.

above When Plan A and Plan B fail, there's always Plan C.

Elements like controlling the controllables (Chapter 6), maintaining a positive attitude (Chapter 9) or simply grinding out a result (Chapter 12). However, the athlete has to have both the confidence and the right mindset to be able to do that; it is all too easy to write a race off as a 'bad' day. Of course, bad days happen. But with the right attitude and preparation, the athlete should still be able to realise a result even if they are having one of 'those' days. It is simply a question of working out what variables need to change to turn a bad day into an acceptable one. When the athlete can do that, they can rest assured that they have gained control over both the body and the mind.

ADAPTATION: KEY POINTS

- How you respond to the variables beyond your control will often determine the outcome of your race.
- Endurance sports require thought and strategy. Sometimes it is better to be defensive than offensive (until the end of the race).
- Be prepared to compromise and improvise if you want to realise your goals – perfect days are few and far between.
- Formulate a Plan A and Plan B for a race. If racing in extreme conditions, have a Plan C, just in case.

11

Microgoalling:
How do you eat an elephant?

There is a large psychological difference between swimming one mile in a pool and one mile in a straight line. If you stand on the edge of a pool with a view to swimming a mile, your mind breaks the physical effort down into lengths. If you stand on the edge of a body of water and look at the finish line in the distance, there is a chance that your mind will baulk at how far a mile actually is to swim.

The same is true for every race. If you stand at the start of a marathon or cyclosportive and think about the fact that you are about to run 42.2 kilometres or cycle 200 kilometres it can seem like a very long way. However, if you break up that distance into smaller goals, then all of a sudden the mind has targets that are achievable in the short term. Each one of these targets builds towards the overall goal, and so you have a manageable means of realising your objectives.

Which brings us back to the title of this chapter: how do you eat an elephant? It's a metaphor – or rather a mantra – that is used across the business and sporting world. Look at the elephant as a single entity to eat and it is quite overwhelming. Break the elephant down into 'chunks' and take it one bite at a time, and suddenly it becomes manageable.

In the world of endurance sports, the bite-size 'chunks' that we are referring to are specific segments of an event. Those segments can be discipline-orientated (such as swim, bike, run in triathlon), distance orientated (for instance, 1-kilometre or 10-kilometre chunks) or race orientated (checkpoint to checkpoint). They can also be time-orientated, with athletes setting targets per segment that build towards a predetermined race goal. The key is to focus on a series of targets that will build towards the completion of the race.

For this technique to be truly effective, you would benefit from familiarising yourself with the course. That way, you know the environment that you are racing in (which acts as an immediate confidence booster) and can identify key 'signposts' along the route which will help drive you towards your goal. However, if this is not possible, you can still glean motivational benefits from this strategy by researching the course ahead of time. Very few races withhold courses and routes from athletes; if they do so usually these courses are revealed

the night before the event. Studying the course – even on paper – will allow you to identify checkpoints, markers or feed stations in a race that you can target en route to the finish line.

And this is from a very 'top-level' race planning and strategy perspective.

As we are about to see, when severely fatigued it is possible to be even more granular; breaking a race down into mini segments with tangible goals that would ordinarily be ignored on the journey to the finish line. By doing this, you are not only developing an effective race strategy, but also setting yourself realistic targets that may help you to push through a bad patch or overcome a period of extreme fatigue.

Breaking down the *ultra*
RYAN SANDES

Ryan Sandes has carved a formidable reputation for himself in the ultra-marathon community. In a relatively short space of time Sandes has recorded a win at the legendary Leadville 100, a clean sweep of the 4 Deserts ultra-marathon series (he is the only competitor to have won all four races), and numerous course records at both single and multi-stage events around the world. It is an impressive resume for someone who only entered his first marathon as an excuse to 'have a party' back in 2008.

Having caught the running bug, Sandes spent a year entering trail races around his native South Africa before stumbling across the 4 Deserts website. For those unfamiliar with one of the hardest ultra-marathon race series in the world, the 4 Deserts is a series of races across the world's toughest deserts: the Atacama, the Gobi, the Sahara and Antarctica. Taking place over seven days and made up of approximately 250 kilometres, these self-supported races are designed to

left Breaking a race down into 'bitesize' phases will make it easier to tackle.

test the mettle of the most hardened athletes. Sandes reflects:

❝ **I only ever planned** on doing one ultra-marathon, particularly in the weeks leading up to the race. I was so sick of all of the training that I wanted to go back to having a bit of a social life again and hanging out with my friends.

But the race went really well, I really enjoyed it. There was a feeling of fulfilment when I crossed the finishing line; fulfilment at just finishing such a big challenge. I think that is one of the things I enjoy most about ultra-running: it's a test of your endurance but also your mental strength. I think you can learn a hell of a lot about yourself when you're running 100 miles and things aren't going your way – you learn about what you're made of.

Endurance races don't get much more raw than self-supported multi-stage, ultra-running events. Athletes are expected to carry everything they need for the duration of the race except water. Makeshift camps are erected at the end of every stage with basic facilities on offer to participants. Of course, doctors are on hand to monitor the progress of individuals and deal with everyday problems (such as severe blistering), and occasionally there will be

below Ultra marathon running is endurance sport in its rawest form.

qualified physiotherapists to help soothe various aches and pains. However, for all intents and purposes athletes are left alone to manage their body and its recovery in incredibly challenging environments.

From deserts to jungles, high-altitude mountain races to Arctic tundra, competitors in ultra-marathon races are expected to run back-to-back stages that almost always exceed marathon distances (the longest ultra in the world – the Self-Transcendence 3,100 Mile Race – features 52 days of 60-mile stages running around a single block in New York). Regardless of the surrounds, the stress that this places on the body is considerable. As such, the need to manage the mind's reaction to that stress is paramount.

Throughout his career, Ryan Sandes has refined a technique that he believes is essential for any endurance athlete completing a long-distance challenge: microgoalling.

" **I think a lot** of athletes do it – if you look at Ironman or triathlon you're always focusing on getting through one discipline and on to the next. But if you look at running – which is only one discipline – I find that it helps to break up the race if I go from one checkpoint to the next. A lot of people do it – I think a lot do it subconsciously.

By breaking up the race into mini-chunks you are able to stay in a positive frame of mind, which is important. As soon as you get into a negative frame of mind and you're not enjoying it then that is when things are going to go bad. I've often seen people going into a race and thinking: 'How am I going to get through seven days? It's really hot out there and I'm going to suffer, I don't like running in sand' and they have a terrible race. Sure, running in the sand and extreme heat over seven days is hard work, but you've got to see it as a challenge and you've got to be excited to tackle that challenge. Obviously you're going to have the highs and lows, but how you deal with those lows is how you're going to get through the race.

By breaking up a race into lots of mini-chunks you

can stay positive and you can stay focused. If you're focusing on running one kilometre at a time then you can say 'I've run 20 kilometres now, another 30 kilometres to go.' Then 21 kilometres is ticked off and so it continues. It's almost like you feel like you're achieving something the whole time and working towards that bigger goal.

The key to the successful execution of a strategy based on microgoalling is familiarisation with a course. To enable him to do this, Sandes will base himself at an event site in the weeks leading up to a race. This allows him to both acclimatise to the surroundings and familiarise himself with the route. He makes sure he knows where all of the checkpoints are and, if possible, will run most of the course as part of his preparation. This familiarisation has two ostensible benefits: the first is that Sandes becomes comfortable with the course and the surroundings, giving him the confidence to focus purely on his performance come race day; the second is that this knowledge allows him to develop a strategy based on the 'segments' of a race, rather than the race as a whole.

" **I definitely go** into a race with a plan and definitely will focus and break it down and focus on getting through the different checkpoints. Some checkpoints might be 8 kilometres apart and others 24 kilometres – it all depends. But obviously it depends on how I'm feeling between those checkpoints.

The distance and physicality of an ultra-marathon (with many of the courses designed to be as difficult as possible) dictates that they will place significant demands on both the physical and mental strength of the athletes. Once again, this is where Sandes's strategy of microgoalling comes to the fore.

opposite The ultra road is a long one ...

❝ *Say I get through* the first two checkpoints and I'm feeling great, and then I hit a low patch between checkpoints three and four. Once I get to checkpoint four I can put it behind me and say 'I've been there and done that.' It's almost like I feel a lot better once I am past that checkpoint and I'm running a new section of the race. I can put that bad patch behind me.

As mentioned, sometimes checkpoints can be a considerable distance apart. And as anyone who has competed in endurance events knows, there are times when completing one, two or five kilometres seems like an impossibility – let alone 20 kilometres. Once again, Sandes is able to overcome these periods in a race – they are generally periods when the body requires nutrition or hydration – by microgoalling. However, rather than focusing on the next checkpoint when times are hard, Sandes adopts an even more granular approach to his race, focusing on tangible objectives within his immediate surrounds. He found himself practising this technique in the Gobi Desert during his first ultra-marathon, and maintains its validity to this day.

❝ *I was so focused* on trying to stick with the guy in front of me on the long stage that I wasn't eating and drinking enough – I was really out of it. I wasn't that experienced then. The competitive side of me just took over and I was hell-bent on sticking with him – I didn't care if I passed out or died out there, I just had to do everything I could to hold on to that guy. That was really tough for me. When you're in those kind of conditions you have to focus on the really small chunks of a race – almost putting one foot in front of the next – and not get too far ahead of yourself. You just have to focus on getting to the next rock or the next tree or getting to the top of the hill.

Tangible goals when the mind is fatigued are invaluable. Most athletes are racing against an abstract target: time. And while time targets can be an excellent source of motivation going into a race and when a race is going well, when things are difficult or those targets are being missed then time can become the enemy of the athlete. In these instances, having tangible objectives on a course (like trees, points of interest or feed stations) that an athlete can look at, aim for, and pass keeps the individual moving forward. This is essential.

There are races, though, when checkpoints or tangible objectives are not so easy to come by. As part of the 4 Deserts series, Sandes competed in – and won – the Last Desert, the only multi-stage day, multi-stage race on the Antarctic continent. Unlike any other race in the series (or possibly the world), the Last Desert is a completely unknown entity for competitors and organisers alike. While many ultra-marathons do not reveal the route of the race until the night before the event, the organisers of the Last Desert cannot. They are entirely beholden to the weather and the whim of Antarctica, and so competitors spend multiple days out at sea (accommodation is on a boat) as organisers determine which of ten possible locations will be run by the competitors . Even then, the amount of time competitors have to run, and the course they run on, is entirely flexible.

❝ *What made Antarctica* so hard was that it was a completely different race. You live off a boat for the ten days that you're out there. There are so many different factors to deal with. For instance, some of the guys got seasick, which obviously plays on your mind. Also, nothing is too planned because of the weather. So you're off an island and the weather is bad and you could be sitting around for 12 hours, then all of a sudden an announcement comes through on the loudspeaker that says 'you're going to start stage one in three hours'. You just don't have time to prepare.

In most races you run from point A to B so you are running a distance. In Antarctica you run in times. So instead of running A to B you're running a whole bunch of circuits for an amount of time. They do that because the weather changes so frequently. So some of the days we would do 8.5- to 15-kilometre loops, but other days we would do 1.5-kilometre loops. You feel like a hamster going around and around.

Also, once or twice during the race we got pulled off a stage early, which means you never really know how to pace yourself. If you're running 40 kilometres you know what pace to go at – the same with 100 kilometres. But if you don't know whether you're going to be out for one or five hours you don't know how to prepare. One day we got pulled out after an hour. We had clear blue skies one minute, and the next there was a massive storm and you couldn't see five metres ahead of you.

The Last Desert was unconventional and you couldn't control anything. In a race like that you want to have everything pre-planned, but you just have to go with the flow. As an athlete you have to deal with that.

Even in adverse conditions, Sandes was able to call on his strategy of microgoalling to realise his race ambitions.

❝ **We were running** laps so I was focusing on trying to get through one lap at a time, almost shutting out everything around me and focusing on that one lap and then the next. You also had to gauge your strategy – as I said they told us we would be out there for 12 hours but I would estimate eight – so I would run at a pace according to that. You would have to run within yourself in case you were out for the full time. Mentally, I just tried to shut out everything around me and take it one lap at a time. I almost had to pretend to myself that I was only running was one lap and that was it. I just had to be able to deal with that.

It was an effective strategy in a tough race. With the format of the race slightly altered due to the changing nature of the conditions in Antarctica, Sandes won the event by covering more ground than his nearest rival.

right When things get really tough just focus on a tangible goal.

left In some environments it is impossible to have a game plan.

In fact, over the seven days that the Last Desert was run, Sandes completed 230.5 kilometres. That was an enormous 36.6 kilometres further than anyone else in the 2010 edition of the race. Aside from in 2006, when the organisers were able to run the race as planned, Sandes's effort in 2010 remains by far the furthest any athlete has managed to run during the Last Desert race.

Sandes's ability to do so is testament not only to his formidable mental strength, but also his adherence to a race-day strategy that enables him to cope with every variable – both in terms of the race and his body's reaction to it.

Endurance events take place over extended courses and periods of time. What's more, they are hard. As we have seen repeatedly throughout this book, the way an athlete approaches a race, from a mental perspective, will have a profound impact on his or her performance during that event. As such, microgoalling is a relatively simple but undoubtedly effective way of tackling a race. Not only does it make an event taking place over multiple miles, and sometimes days, seem infinitely more manageable, but it can also help the athlete through the difficult spells that are part and parcel of pushing the body to its physical limits.

MICROGOALLING: KEY POINTS

- Break a race down into predetermined 'chunks' to give yourself a psychological edge.
- When struggling in a race situation, focus on tangible objectives while trying to rectify any deficiencies or problems.
- Learn how to put a difficult section behind you and focus on the next 'chunk' of a race.

12

The grind:
Pushing on through

Hang around enough races, take part in enough training sessions or talk to enough endurance athletes and you will eventually hear about 'grinding'. The grind is many things to many people, but at its crux it is the ability to push on through when things are mentally and/or physically tough. It is those sessions – or even periods of time – when fatigue kicks in, perhaps motivation is low, and the athlete feels like they are suffering. Every endurance athlete – regardless of their ability or the level at which they play their sport – is familiar with the grind and will at some point be forced to grind their way through a session or even a race.

As such, developing the mental toughness to push on when things get hard becomes an essential skill for endurance athletes to master. As we discovered in Chapter 1 (What is mental toughness?), mental toughness is an ethereal concept that is difficult to define. However, the definitions produced by both athletes and psychologists tend to centre on the ability to overcome adversity. In the context of endurance sports that means being able to embrace the suffering that is part and parcel of the pursuit.

If we accept that endurance athletes will experience periods of suffering as part of their sport, then a key element to success must be an athlete's ability to deal with that suffering. Some athletes respond positively to it, employing strategies and techniques to manage their pain. Others let the pain of training or competition defeat them. These athletes might not be mentally 'weak', instead, they may simply not know how to deal with the onset of pain in their body. As a result, when the pain begins to 'bite', their mind may adopt a defensive strategy which could lead to them under-performing as they grind their way to the finish line (if they finish at all).

Learning to manage pain is therefore one of the key goals for any endurance athlete. The first step to realising that goal is accepting the pain, rather than being 'scared' of it.

Listening to your body and your *mind*

Try to identify your mental and physical responses to the onset of pain. What is your mind thinking? What is it telling your body to do? What do

Mike
HALL

" You go everywhere that you can really go in your own internal thoughts throughout the process and then when you're getting towards the end you've only really got the dangerous thoughts you've tried to hide along the way.

you think and say to yourself to keep moving forward? As soon as you can start to identify and recognise the thought processes adopted by your mind during periods of physical discomfort then you can begin to develop strategies for coping with that pain.

Many times, difficult patches in a race are just that: patches. They come just as quickly as they go. For the most part they will reflect a shortfall in an aspect of your race-day strategy. That shortfall might be nutrition- or hydration-related, or could be the consequence of environmental factors (heat, cold, etc.). If you were in the position to take a step back during that bad patch and evaluate the situation from a logical point of view, then you would probably be able to determine what you needed to do to recover the situation. However, in the physically and mentally fatigued moment it is not so easy to adopt a logical perspective on suffering. As a result, it is not impossible that a bad patch might destroy your race.

If, however, you are familiar with the early signs of pain and know historically how you have dealt with

left You have to learn that pain is an inevitable part of the endurance sport experience

below Nutrition and hydration are key to overcoming difficult 'patches'

above Learn to develop coping mechanisms when a race becomes tough

issues during the training phase of your preparation, then you can employ positive coping mechanisms (see Chapter 9 on self-talk) alongside addressing any nutrition and hydration issues. So while the difficult periods of a race will still be difficult, because you have identified your thought processes during these periods you can welcome them and then start to overcome them. Coping mechanisms will not make the pain go away, but they will enable the mind – and as a direct result the body – to deal with difficult parts of a race.

Once the mind is back in control, then it is up to you to start grinding.

The ultimate *grind*
MIKE HALL

The majority of endurance athletes follow a similar path through their chosen sport: they decide they want to pursue a sport; they then sign up to a race; they train for that race; they race; they then (hopefully) sign up for another season and start analysing where improvements in their performance can be made.

Most endurance athletes follow that route, but not all. There are a small number of races that are so demanding that an individual will tackle them once – maybe a handful of times, at best – in a lifetime. What's more, the nature of these challenges are so extreme that training for them is an exploratory process that begins before the race and continues throughout its duration.

In 2009 Mike Hall was a competitive racer on the endurance mountain-bike scene (long-distance and 24-hour races). Realising that he performed better in long-distance races, Hall's interest was piqued by an event called the Tour Divide. A self-supported 2,700-mile race from Canada to Mexico, the Tour Divide is one of a growing number of punishing ultra-endurance bike races that test the mental and physical strength of athletes around the world. Hall decided to enter the race, and in 2011 responded well to the demands of the event.

> ❝ **I went into** that race with no expectations but surprised myself a little bit and managed to hang on to the back of the leaders for a while until I got injured. I found out that the longer the race the better I went.

Despite succumbing to injury during the race, Hall completed the event in 19 days. After that, it was a question of what next? As might be expected, he chose to play to his strengths and looked long. In fact, he looked very long.

> ❝ **The race around** the world was the longest I had heard of and I thought I could do pretty well in it so I got some good support organised with sponsorship and threw myself into it.

Having committed to cycling around the world, Hall began training. In particular, he addressed the areas that had affected his race during the Tour Divide, before going on to build up his raw bike strength through pure time in the saddle.

> ❝ **The Tour Divide** was good training in itself really, and speaking to people who had done that before they said that your form carries through – it's not something that leaves you very quickly.
>
> So from June until February I was just working on making myself strong and strengthening my tendons because they were the things that got injured first. I wanted to work on those so had about three months off and then I started again with some high mileage. After that I started training on a fixed-wheel track bike

and went and found as many steep hills as I could. That gave me the strength in my muscles but also the strength in my connective tissue so when you're pulling on it day after day it stands up to it. My main weakness in the Tour Divide was in the tendons so that's what I concentrated on.

I knew that I had the endurance from before and that wasn't going to go anywhere and that if anything I could train into the event. You can either show up fit and go off from the gun or you can build up to it so I thought I would be alright whatever happened really.

Originally, the World Cycle Races Grand Tour (as it was eventually known) had been set up as a fully organised self-supported race around the world. However, in the end participants settled on simply making a gentleman's agreement to race one another, play by the rules, and complete the event as outlined by the Guinness Book of Records (cyclists must complete a 24,900-mile/40,073-kilometre circumnavigation of the globe, of which 18,000 miles/28,968 kilometres must be covered on bike). Ten men set off from Greenwich on 18 February 2012, and apart from a few chance meetings and regular communication on social networking sites that was pretty much the last Hall would see of them.

> ❝ **We all had** different routes and went from different ferry ports so literally past the gates of Greenwich we were on our own. A few of them went to the same ferry port but I took a completely different one to everyone else.

So began an epic race around the world. Over the course of 107 days Hall clocked up 91 days and 18 hours' cycling time and an astonishing 200 miles per day, covering 18,000 miles in total and smashing Alan Bate's previous world record of 106 days, 10 hours and 33 minutes, set over a 127-day period. It was a remarkable achievement from a man with relatively little multi-day, ultra-endurance riding experience. Needless to say, during the course of his 91-day circumnavigation of the globe, Hall was forced to call on his ability to grind out

above Mike Hall overcame numerous physical issues during his round-the-world cycle

the miles on an almost daily basis (the only times that he wasn't riding were port-to-port transit days). He had objectives for each day, although he was careful not to let his strategy to beat the record become too rigid.

"*I didn't really want* to write a plan because I didn't want to be stuck to it. If I was doing well I didn't want to back off and if I wasn't doing well I didn't want it to hurt my morale.

In the end I wrote a schedule. A lot of people were saying 80 days because it's a nice number. I knew it was probably out of reach but I thought that if I wrote it to that and aspired to it then I wouldn't beat myself up if I didn't make it but it would also give me something to chase. So I could be chasing it and failing but at the same time doing better than I thought I ever could.

Importantly, Hall was very careful with whom he shared this schedule.

"*I had this plan* that I wouldn't share with anyone. That was a big thing, actually. The more people who knew about it the more pressure I felt to try and meet it and that wasn't the point of it. It was something for me to push myself with, not for other people to push me with. There were a few people that I shared it with, people who I felt knew me, knew the race or who had helped me with my preparation, but it was a small handful of people and they knew as well as I did that I wasn't expecting to meet it. Four out of five days I maybe met the mileage or it was better than I thought I could do, so it helped.

Keeping those miles ticking over were essential to Hall's eventual success. To average the 200 miles per day that he had targeted, he formed a routine that he adhered to on a daily basis.

❝ **Mentally it's best** to get the miles done in the morning – you feel a lot happier about it. You don't want to be making up the miles at the end of the day and riding late into the night.

Getting up and getting in the early miles, I had a target of the first 100 by three o'clock. That told me that I could then finish another 100 miles between 10 p.m. and midnight. Sometimes I wouldn't quite make it and I had just had a stop before that or something else happened. Other days I would make the first 100 by about 1.30 p.m.

Each day it would normally work out that I could be up between 4.30 a.m. and 5 a.m. In the latter stages it would take me nearly an hour to get up and riding again. Then I would immediately get ready with breakfast – I think I once did 30 miles with no food and it was horrible, I was literally crawling – there is no value in doing anything else except trying to eat in the morning. I think that's why it took a while to get to those first 100 miles in, because in the morning I would always be trying to eat. Sometimes I would get to a place to eat before I started, but more often than not I would need to stop a couple of times in the morning. If

I had made the 100 miles by 3 p.m. I would give myself a stop depending on where I was and eat again and then I wouldn't really need to eat until about 8 p.m. if the weather was good and I was riding well I could do another 50 miles and go on until 11 p.m. or midnight. And that was it really, the daily routine. It was all about riding and getting food.

Hall's schedule was gruelling, and contained few rest days. He averaged around 15mph for the duration of the race, receiving scant return for any additional effort he made to push harder. As such, it became a matter of managing his body and mind and its response to the sustained effort.

❝ **Food picks you up** mentally because it just seems to take the aches away and make you feel fresher, but you can't stop all the time so you've got to find the balance between stopping and spending long hours on the bike.

Perhaps as important as fuelling, Hall was constantly looking for ways to deal with the aches, pains and injuries that blighted his performance. Crossing Australia he picked up a bug that weakened him, leaving him 'shuffling on' in a bid to keep to his targets. Meanwhile, throughout the duration of the journey he wrestled with a loss of feeling in his hands due to the pressure of resting on them day after day.

❝ **My left hand** went numb after the first week and it was pretty much numb all the way through India. That's because I had so much pressure on my hands – I found it difficult to find positions in which I wasn't putting a lot of pressure on them. I could grip the hoods for a while but the vibration would come through the hoods so I would have to change my grip – I had several different grips. That was quite worrying but when I had a couple of days off in between the feeling would start to come back. When I bought some gel bar tape and

left Hall's bike: exactly what it says on the frame.

above Sometimes the most important thing is to simply keep moving forward.

gel gloves it started to come back a bit more. There was always a bit of a tingling though, and even after I came back I had it for a while as nerve damage takes a month or so to repair.

His hands weren't the only issue. As he had experienced during the Tour Divide, Hall also struggled with his tendons throughout his journey. And like the problems with his hands, Hall realised the he was faced with two choices: pushing on through the aches and pains or quitting.

" **I knew that** it wasn't an injury unless I let it become an injury. I knew I could manage it and there were things I could do to stop it.

With my tendons I could tape my heels up and give that support to my Achilles. And I learnt a technique for doing that which worked: putting my saddle down a lot; not a lot in one go but many times. So after about two or three days I would need to drop my saddle three to five millimetres and then after another five days I would need to drop it again. It just felt like I was putting it down and down. Each time I was unconvinced it was going to work as I thought 'How far can I keep putting the saddle down?' But every time I put the saddle down not only did it stop the pain getting worse, but within a day it was getting better. So in the morning after 50 miles with chronic stiffness coming up through my legs, I would put the saddle down and ride 100 miles and it would be getting better with every pedal stroke.

Of course, physiotherapists around the globe would baulk at the assertion that you can ride through these injuries. And of course, any athlete who is experiencing sustained physical discomfort should look to address those problems with qualified medical professionals. But Hall was in a relatively unique position. Not only was he part of an extraordinary race, but he was leading it in a time that would give him a world record. What's more, he felt physically capable of riding through injuries that he did not believe were too serious.

> ❝ **You can ride** and ride and as long as it isn't getting worse – and you know if it is because it gets worse very quickly – you can almost pedal through it. Riding it will keep it moving and warm it up and you can recover from the injury while doing high mileage. It's not something I ever thought I could do, and you realise it's not a case of your leg starts hurting and you stop. You can manage it as you go but you have to keep trying things. Some of the problems I had in my shoulders and back got better the more I went. Those things can cause you a lot of anxiety and you can sit there and think 'My leg's hurting' and it makes you feel like stopping. I learnt in America the year before that it doesn't get bad and then keep getting worse until you stop. It gets bad and then it can get better.

Hall adopted a pragmatic approach to dealing with his injuries, and one that was necessary if he was going to realise his goals. However, it wasn't just the aches and pains of the body that he had to overcome. Hall also needed to manage his mind through the process.

During the course of the race Hall basically rode solo, meaning that he had a lot of time with few distractions. This proved to be one of the most challenging aspects of the race.

> ❝ **It's really nice** when your mind can wander off and you're not thinking that your hands are going numb or your back aches. But that can be quite tough when you've gone through all the thought processes and you've thought of everything you usually think of. Music can be a good distraction in that sense. You want to try and daydream a little bit and take your mind somewhere else, then come back a couple of hours later and find that you've done 30 miles or something. That's the best scenario but it's often hard to get there. It's like when you go to sleep; the best thing you want is an empty mind and you want to drift off. If you sit there saying 'I want to get to sleep' it never happens. That's the same thing, you're there going 'my hands hurt' or 'this hurts' and you're constantly reminded of what's bothering you, rather than being distracted from it.

Needless to say on a journey as long and physically demanding as the one Mike Hall undertook, it became more and more difficult to find distractions for his mind. In fact, as he neared his goal – and the record – Hall struggled to contain the negative thoughts that plagued his mind.

> ❝ **I was mentally** completely blown out. You go everywhere that you can really go in your own internal thoughts throughout the process and then when you're getting towards the end you've only really got the dangerous thoughts you've tried to suppress along the way. So you think 'What would happen if I did just chuck it all in?' It's strange but you've occupied your mind all of the way through and you run out of positive things to think of.
>
> Towards the end I was getting to the point where I was entertaining the bad thoughts more than the good. I just didn't have anything more to think about. I had pushed them away a lot until then, but I started to give them more time. In some ways, when you've been doing that for three months you think it's all a bit pointless. Those are the dangerous thoughts, thinking about the bigger picture and wondering if it means anything and 'I've been doing this for this long and it seems a bit stupid', rather than suppressing that and getting on with what you had decided to do when you left and when you were in your right mind.

Under the weight of fatigue and – to some extent – because of the solitary nature of his pursuit, Hall had started to crack.

> ❝ **I knew that I** just needed to get home before I completely lost the plot.

Still, though, he pushed on. Where some would have quit having covered an admirable amount of land in a relatively short space of time, Hall grinded it out even though his body and mind were ready to stop. Grinding it out was in fact very much the way he managed the entire race. From the off he was focused on constantly moving forward, always hitting – or coming as close as he physically could to – his goals.

❝ *I would feel guilty* if I stopped. Thinking back to when I started the USA section – because I didn't want to think about the record until then – through the States I wanted to do 200 miles a day. That's when that became my daily target and I would feel like I wasn't on plan or comfortable if I hadn't made that. Even when I was sick in Australia I didn't want to stop for a day because I needed to feel like I was still moving.

At the start, because of the pressure of the race you do everything at race speed. So you're brushing your teeth at that speed and going to bed early to get up early – you're living at a race pace. That sets the tone for the rest of it. Even though it slows down and takes a little bit longer to get into and out of bed or onto the bike or your stops take 40 minutes instead of half an hour, with that slowing down you're still trying to achieve what you were achieving before but it's just slightly slowed down.

But you do end up when you're very tired, stopping and when you've eaten something looking at the empty plate in a daze. That's the danger sign. You suddenly realise what you are doing and you snap out of it and say 'Come on, I've got to get on with this.' My thing was that if I wasn't eating or sleeping I should be riding. You always try to make it so you can do two things at once. So if I met anyone on the road and they wanted to chat it was always fine as long as I was eating at the same time or something like that.

Idle moments do creep in the longer you go. I think that is what most wore me out mentally: you don't realise how much time you need during your day just to do nothing. Without all those little idle moments it

above Sometimes it's important to clear the head of all thoughts.

makes it a really intense and stressful way of life. You don't just have five minutes to look out the window and do nothing. Every single moment of your time is filled. I think that's what drains you – not having those moments to reflect or let your mind do nothing.

Of course, Hall's singular determination to achieve the goals that he had established for himself is not only impressive but relatively unique. Hall managed to push his body and mind further and faster than anyone in the history of cycling. What's more, he did it with little in the way of incentive – like so many endurance events there was nothing on the line other than pride and the ability to say 'I did that'. It was a truly impressive feat and one that deserves its place in the record books. What's more, as well as claiming a world record, Hall can lay bona fide claim to having completed the ultimate grind.

Elite athletes: pushing the *limits*

Most endurance athletes can pinpoint a race, session or challenge where they have had to grind out a result. This grind is an almost inevitable consequence of pushing their own mental and physical limits. However, part of the motivation for pushing on through a tough session or difficult race is realising the benefits that this can afford in the long run.

In December 2010 William Trubridge became the first man to swim below 100m in the Constant Weight Without Fins discipline of freediving. In a sport where there are numerous categories of competition for different types of dives, Constant Weight Without Fins sees divers reach depths with no aids (such as dive sledges, weights or fins). As Trubridge himself explains, it is 'the purest form of freediving and the purest form of what we're capable of doing underwater'. It was a remarkable feat of human endurance and demanded absolute control over the body and mind to master what can be a dangerous sport.

Of course, it has taken Trubridge years to reach the level of control required to realise such significant depths. Like every athlete, he has good days and bad. Crucially, though, when things aren't quite going to plan he uses the bad days to develop his abilities to manage his mind.

below Every endurance athlete will have to grind out a race or training session.

❝ **You have days** when you're not in top shape. Normally in training I try to force through that to an extent. You don't want to be silly about it – if you're feeling completely awful you don't want to try for a personal best.

But if you always submit to calling off a dive because you don't feel 100 per cent then you go down a route to being more and more lazy and getting more controlled by your mood, superstition, or any of the things that cause you to get stressed out or not feel your best. I try to push through that, and sometimes my best dives have been when I haven't felt too motivated or been in top shape but I've done the dive anyway and felt more confident afterwards. That's a really important part of my training: trying to increase confidence through those occasions.

Trubridge's view on the importance of grinding out a training session is echoed by South African ultra-marathon runner Ryan Sandes and his perspective on racing.

❝ **I always want** to push those boundaries in every race. When you get to that stage I suppose you've mentally been able to overpower the physical side of your body. It's that fine line between pushing yourself over the edge and being able to ride on the crest of a wave.

There have been times I have really pushed myself beyond my limits. I think the first time I had to do it was during the long stage of the Gobi Desert

below You can experience your strongest days when you don't feel like racing.

above The best in the world often grind out wins when they're not in top shape.

[see page 130]. You've got to really be focused. Pushing those limits has a big mental side to it and for me that competitive side of me takes over.

Managing the mind and its suffering, and in particular taking control of the thoughts that are telling you to stop – the 'dangerous' thoughts, as Mike Hall describes them – is an essential tool for every endurance athlete to master. There will be times when it is raining or when you are tired or life is getting in the way and you will simply not want to go out and train. Similarly, if you take part in enough races you will have days where you feel 'flat', or simply not up to the task at hand. And while the mind might do everything that it can to make you feel like that is the case, it is important to recognise that, for the most part, it is not the reality of the situation. If you have done the training and prepared as well as you can then your body is capable of so much more than your mind sometimes wants you to believe. At that point, pushing through that barrier becomes essential.

THE GRIND: KEY POINTS

- Endurance sports invariably involve degrees of suffering. Be prepared to suffer and embrace the pain of the sport.
- Identify how your body and mind respond to suffering (thoughts, feelings, etc.). Use that identification on race day to help push you through tough patches.
- The body is not always as fatigued as the mind sometimes believes. It's amazing how many steps you can take in the time it takes to think 'I can't take one more step'.
- You can sometimes realise the best outcomes on days when you do not want to train or race. Do not always succumb to days when you just don't feel like it.

13

Winning:
It's all in the mind

It's almost a given that to succeed in sport you have to be motivated either by a desire to win or a desire to compete. In fact, it would seem counter-intuitive to suggest otherwise. But before we begin a discussion on the mentality of winning, it is important to point out that there are many endurance athletes – some of whom are bona fide winners or pioneers of their sports – who do not consider themselves competitive.

As discussed in Chapter 2 (Motivation: Keeping the fire burning), many athletes who compete in endurance sports are not motivated by winning. Rather, they are motivated by a desire to push their physical limits. In fact, in terms of competition, they get greater pleasure from challenging these limits than they do by defeating an opponent (although plenty take a lot of pleasure in that too). Ultra-marathon runner Dean Karnazes exemplifies this attitude.

> **To me,** it's you against you so I'm never really competing against other people. I've always competed against myself. Even in some of the most competitive races that I've been in it's not about winning but more about the journey. It's always been that way to me.
>
> I've read a lot about sport psychology and there's a famous quote that says: 'If you don't mind losing you'll never win.' I don't know if I agree with that altogether because I don't mind losing and I have won. Maybe not as much as others who are so dead-set on winning that that's their driving motivation. I know many athletes like that and they are great, great champions in terms of medals. But a lot of them burn out because you can't keep that up forever.
>
> At a point there has to be an internal passion because you can only win for so long no matter how good you are. So for me it's always been about the adventure and the journey and not necessarily the winning. And when I do win it's just me being the best me that I can be.

Karnazes has won races. In fact, he's won some of the world's toughest ultra-marathon races (including the legendary Badwater Ultramarathon). However, during the course of his career he has also set himself a variety of individual challenges that are beyond the physical capabilities of most individuals. These challenges have ranged from running 350 miles non-

Stephen ROCHE

> You should never say the sky is the limit. Once you say the sky is the limit you're putting a limit on what you can do.

stop to completing a successful 3,000-mile run from Anaheim to New York – across the USA – in 75 days (averaging between 40 and 50 miles per day). He is often the only competitor in these 'races', and as such has repeatedly demonstrated that he is motivated by things other than simply winning.

Like Karnazes, Dee Caffari is an athlete who is fundamentally motivated by the challenge that endurance sports afford her. Interestingly, though, she believes that she has 'evolved' as a competitor. Originally attracted to trans-Oceanic sailing by the sheer challenge of the pursuit, she recognises that competition has helped to maintain her motivation.

> ❝ **I'm definitely someone** who has evolved. When I set off the wrong way round it was about adventure and being the first woman to do something. I took an opportunity that presented itself. It was about completing it and I learnt a lot along the way. Now my sailing has evolved and I'm in a competitive arena and now it is about performance. I've ticked the boxes, I've got some world records and I've delivered. But now I've upped my game and want to put myself where the big boys are.

Something drives endurance athletes to push themselves further and faster. Competition is undoubtedly at the heart of that. But what is it competition against? For some, it is the traditional concept of an athlete-against-athlete tussle to get to the finish line first. For others, the competition is much more personal. It is about pushing their limits and challenging themselves. If they can do that, they have 'won' their race.

There are however a group of athletes who make a career out of winning. In fact, they are prepared to go to extraordinary lengths to do so.

left Not every endurance athlete is motivated by winning.

Winning

Very good athletes win from time to time. The very best athletes win consistently and they win when it matters. They are known around the world as being the best at what they do, and their names are familiar even to individuals who take little if any interest in sport. They are athletes like Roger Federer, Michael Phelps or Muhammad Ali.

What separates the very good from the very best? 'Their drive, their determination, their confidence in their own ability. We all have confidence and we all have drive but these guys would not accept defeat most times.' Those are the words of a man who has not only ridden alongside some of the best cyclists in the history of road cycling, but has been instrumental in helping propel them to victory: George Hincapie. During the course of a formidable 19-year career, Hincapie was one of the lead *domestiques* for both Alberto Contador (2007) and Cadel Evans (2011) during their Tour de France wins. He was also the only *domestique* to ride with Lance Armstrong during every one of his now erased seven Tour de France 'wins'.

As such, he knows the traits and characteristics of cycling winners.

❝ **I would say** the drive. Many guys reach a good level in the sport and they start to rely on only their talent. The sport is so hard that not only do you have to rely on your talent you have to sacrifice day in and day out and count every calorie and push yourself to the limit every day. When you start letting that go, that's when it really shows in the sport. You can't do it 90 per cent, you have to do it 110 per cent.

Winning is not easy. The athletes who become the best in the world work tirelessly to get there. They are athletes who study the sport, familiarise themselves with the competition and work religiously to iron out any flaws in their performances. What's more, they believe. They believe in themselves, they believe in

above Winning is not easy.

the talent and the work that they have put in to their performance, and they have an unwavering belief in their ability to win. This belief extends beyond registering occasional victories during the course of the year. True champions of a sport believe that they will win each and every race that they enter, and prepare meticulously to realise that aim.

Of course, all of their personalities are different. So are the intrinsic factors that motivate them to victory. But they all share a drive and ambition to be the best in their sport, and will generally stop at nothing to realise that goal.

The mentality of a **winner**
CRAIG ALEXANDER

It took 12 years for Craig Alexander to become the dominant athlete in Ironman triathlon. During that time – his apprenticeship in the sport – Alexander worked religiously on his physical and mental strength. Having 'arrived' in triathlon at a relatively late age, he took a patient approach to his development, but remained confident that he would reach the levels towards which he aspired.

Of course, he had every reason to be optimistic. Even though he wasn't winning consistently, Alexander was still recording solid results and the occasional victory. These results were proof enough for the Australian that his development was going in the right direction.

" Early in my career my wife used to say to me that she thought it would be beneficial for me to see a sports psychologist. At that point I thought it was a valuable suggestion but I knew it wasn't the right time because I was getting a lot of results from third place through to fifteenth. That was more to do with my physical development – I was playing catch-up to athletes who were at a higher physical level than I was. I still felt like I was performing to my physical potential at the time – it wasn't a lack of mental toughness that wasn't allowing me to break through, I just physically wasn't at the level of Greg Welch, Miles Stewart or Simon Lessing.

below Becoming a winner requires a different mindset.

I knew that it was going to take a few more years to close that last 3 to 5 per cent against guys – guys who are Olympians, world champions, some of the best athletes the sport has seen. They were great athletes and great competitors and they could work you out. They could see where your weaknesses were and they could expose you. It wasn't a mental flaw, just physically I wasn't ready to compete. I'd been in the sport five minutes and some of them had been in the sport a decade and had multiple world titles to their name. So I was always honest and felt that I still had some physical work to do to get on that level.

Hard work and patience have epitomised Alexander's approach to triathlon. What's more, they are the reason why he has not only been phenomenally successful, but is widely regarded as one of the greatest triathletes of all time. He is also a perceptive athlete, and when he felt like he was ready to win he accepted that his approach to the sport would have to change accordingly.

" **When I got** to the point where I felt like I was ready to consistently compete in every race, it required a huge focus on my part to shake off the shackles of being content with third to fifteenth. It's a different mindset to look at a start list and say 'I've beaten all of those guys but on different days' and to go and say 'I need to beat all of these guys on one day – today or tomorrow.' That's a different mentality.

My self-evaluation and self-appraisal was always honest – good or bad – and when I got to the point where I thought 'I'm good enough to win big races consistently' I thought that I had to be mentally ready as well – it's not just physical. You hear a million stories of athletes who are world champions in training but can't translate that performance on race day, and I thought 'I don't want to be one of those athletes.'

For me it was very easy. Through my physio degree, I had studied a bit of psychology so I had a fair idea of how the human mind works. My mentality was pretty simple: I have the utmost respect for all the guys that

above Craig Alexander wins the biggest prize in Ironman: Kona.

I race. Early in my career I had a lot of their posters on my wall. People always say that it is hard to beat someone you look up to and that is true. I always looked up to and admired and respected these guys, but I also respected the level of commitment that I put into the sport. And I think my mentality changed from 'Why me, why should I be the one to win?' to 'Why not me? I'm working as hard as these guys, I've trained with a lot of them, at the very least I think I'm on par with them. I respect them immensely and I've learnt a lot from all of them but I think I'm ready to beat them and why shouldn't I be ready? I've trained and I've committed and invested as much time and effort and energy as they have so why not me? Why shouldn't I be the one to win?'

When I look at that physical level I was never timid or shy to win – some people are. And I just thought 'I'm ready.' I had won and I had had a taste – as I said I had won some points races, a few half-Ironmans and beaten some good guys here and there. But to do it consistently and do it all on the same day is a different mentality. I just thought 'This is not personal but I'm here to do the best I can and I'm here to compete with all of these guys.' I always held them in high esteem but above all of that the thing I held in the highest esteem was the commitment and level of devotion that I had given to the sport and I wanted to honour that.

Alexander did so in spectacular style. In a short space of time he went from a regular podium finisher to one of the biggest names in triathlon thanks to a string of impressive victories. In particular, Alexander views his win at the 2005 Lifetime Fitness Triathlon as a breakthrough. The format of the invitational Olympic distance race (1.5km swim, 40km bike, 10km run) was simple: 15 of the best male and female triathletes in the world set off at predetermined, staggered start times to make it a fair battle of the sexes. Against a strong field that included Olympic and half-Ironman champions, Alexander took both the actual win and the equalised win (against the staggered times) by 26 seconds – a huge margin of victory over a relatively short race. It was Alexander's biggest win to date, and it would be the first stepping stone on his way to multiple world championships.

❝ *Winning becomes a habit.* There are so many things you need to unlock mentally. I was able to compartmentalise things. It wasn't personal, it wasn't about me beating this guy or that guy, it was about me performing to the level I knew that I was capable of. So

it wasn't: 'I'm racing Simon Lessing this weekend and I have to beat him.' It was: 'I'm going to perform to the level I know I can.'

It's an interesting distinction but it's an important one: it's always about the performance and not so much the result. Some times you perform out of your skin and out of this world and you get beaten. That's sport. Sometimes you win but the performance hasn't been what your training has indicated that you are capable of. What's more of a success? I guess from an external perspective in terms of the media and prize money and those kinds of things it's important to win because that's when you get recognised, that's when you get prize money and sponsors and that kind of thing. From an intrinsic or a personal point of view it's more about the performance. If you don't perform at the level that your training indicates that you should then something in the system has gone awry. And just because you've won that can mask over inadequacies or deficiencies and that just means that you were better than everyone else. It doesn't mean that you were as good as you could have been.

You look at any sport and the greatest athletes are the ones who are consistent. In sport you aren't going to win all the time. It's impossible. But to bring a consistent level of performance every time is what you aim to do. That's always been my goal.

In many respects, a performance-led approach to winning is similar to Dean Karnazes's perspective on competing against himself. The challenge is to be the 'best me that I can be'. Of course, Alexander is fiercely competitive. He ground out a win at the 2009 Ironman World Championships after a less-than-ideal preparatory phase. But this focus on performance not only continues to act as his primary motivation (he is the oldest champion in the history of the Ironman World Championships), but it keeps him pushing the boundaries of his physical ability, and in turn keeps him winning.

Winning at all *costs*

STEPHEN ROCHE

As Craig Alexander would argue, winning is a mentality. However, not all mentalities are the same. Alexander is motivated by the desire to realise the perfect performance. However, there are also athletes who just want to win. Pure and simple. Stephen Roche is a perfect example of that kind of athlete.

During his 13-year cycling career Stephen Roche racked up an impressive 58 professional wins. However, among cycling aficionados he will always be remembered for one golden year in his career: 1987. During the course of a few short months Roche did what only one other man (the great Eddy Merckx) has managed to do either before him or since: claim the elusive Triple Crown of Cycling. To do that, Roche won the Giro d'Italia, Tour de France and the Road World Cycling Championships. As a standalone achievement it was remarkable, but the manner in which he did it makes it all the more impressive.

Roche won the Giro d'Italia against spectacular odds after being abandoned by most of his team. Early on Stage 15 of the race Roche broke away from the field to launch a solo attack. In so doing, he directly contravened team orders, which were working towards a victory for teammate, race leader and defending Giro champion Roberto Visentini. The move may have propelled Roche towards the Maglia Rosa – and the General Classification win – but it earned him the ire of both the Italian public

---

below Medics had to administer oxygen for 30 minutes before Roche was able to savour his sprint victory.

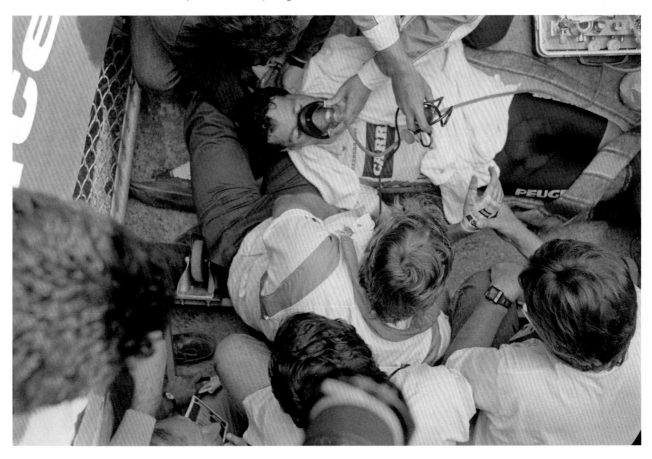

above Roche won the Tour de France in 1987 on the way to completing the Triple Crown of Cycling.

and his teammates (apart from Eddy Schepers who continued to work with the Irishman). Roche and Visentini were involved in a series of clashes on later stages of the Giro, before a crash forced the Italian to retire.

Sealing the win at the Giro d'Italia, Roche immediately jumped in a car and drove to France in preparation for the Tour. During the biggest race in world cycling, he famously buried himself on the mountains

of La Plagne in a bid to close the gap on Tour leader and main rival Pedro Delgado (more on that in Chapter 10 – Adaptation: Improvise to overcome). It worked. A 1-minute, 15-second deficit with 4 kilometres to go was reduced to just four seconds by the end of the now infamous mountain stage. Roche had clawed back enough time on Delgado to overhaul his lead in the General Classification at the time trail at the final stage of the Tour, and the Irishman sealed the yellow jersey in impressive style.

And so it was on to Villach, Austria. Working with his teammate Sean Kelly, Roche managed to jump into a breakaway in the closing kilometres and launched a solo attack with 500 metres to go. In a nail-biting finish the Irishman managed to hold off the group chasing him down to seal the title, and with it the Triple Crown of Cycling.

Over and over again, Roche's victories are the tale of one man repeatedly attacking the field – and his own teammates if necessary – in the pursuit of victory. It is undoubtedly the hardest option in cycling, a sport where a team is usually built around an individual with the goal of delivering that individual to the finish line at the front of the field – or at least ahead of his rivals in the General Classification. Roche paid scant heed to that style of racing.

Admittedly, during his Triple Crown year these aggressive tactics were helped by the lack of communication equipment enjoyed by riders on the Tour today. The Irishman himself acknowledges that the lack of technology helped him catch Delgado in the Tour (and so give him the platform to seal victory in the time trial), and it would have undoubtedly helped him to escape from Visentini in the Giro. But more than technology – or the lack of it – Roche was driven by a ferocious will to win.

❝ **I always said** there was no race small enough to win. Sometimes you can look at a smaller race and say 'I'm in training here' but I was always there saying 'I can win this.' If you win a smaller race it's motivation for the next one, and sometimes the smaller races are harder to win than the big ones. I always thought that there are no medals or prize money for training, so when I was training I trained very, very hard, but I didn't try and compete with the guys that I was training with. When I raced, I raced to win and would settle for doing my best.

I never sat down and said 'this race I want to win, this race whatever', my main thing was that once I put

a number on my back I was a competitor and there was no race too small to win.

Putting Roche's numerous victories down to an unflinching desire to win tells only part of the story. Roche, like any champion, was a student of his sport. He watched, he listened and he learnt about his opponents, their teams and the courses that he rode. The knowledge that he gathered afforded him tactical advantages over his opponents, and allowed him to second-guess the tactics of his rivals and their teams.

❝ **I wasn't just** looking at the road and seeing where I was going. I was also analysing my opponents, looking at what teams have commercial interests in the area – teams always want to perform when they're going through their 'home' lands – so I was always very good at analysing everything, the whole picture, rather than looking at who is second or third and who is going to beat me.

I'm always looking at the other factors in the game. That was always my strong point when I was racing, but also today when I do television analysis or if I'm asked to consult or advise or anything. I take great pride in it. When you talk through a race before it happens and you watch it unfold in a similar way to what you've said then it gives you a boost.

I was always well known as a good tactician because I used to analyse things very widely.

This tactical advantage was then consolidated by the Irishman's unflinching drive to be the best at his sport. What's more, when he references being the best, Roche is very careful to differentiate between what it means to be the best and what it means to try your best. It is a lesson that he uses to motivate his son Nicolas, himself a professional road cyclist.

❝ **When Nicolas** was going to race the Tour of Switzerland I said to him: 'Nicolas how are you going to do?' and he said 'I'm going to do my best.' And I said: 'Then there's no point in going.' 'Why?' he said. 'You go to win, but to do my best is the same, isn't it?' 'It is,' I said, 'but it's not. If you go to do your best you'll be content to finish third or fourth or wherever you finish. If you go to win then you're happy because you've done your best.'

If you go out there to do your best you're not really putting your neck on the line. If you go out there and say 'I'm going to win' you're putting your neck on the line. So if you're in the situation where you might come second, you will give yourself a harder drive because you've told everyone – including yourself – that you're going to win. So you can't just settle for second place. It's very important to set your sights high. I always say that you should never say the sky is the limit. Once you say the sky is the limit you're putting a limit on what you can do.

Roche's perspective on winning might seem relatively straightforward, but it is far from it. Like every sporting champion he was rigorous in both his physical and mental preparation. Going into a race he was always confident that he had done everything that he could to give himself the best chance of winning it. These are the traits that he believes define winners.

❝ **They are people** who are very meticulous – they don't leave any stone unturned. They go down to fine detail. A lot of people have the same physical ability but they haven't got the same mental ability, they can't structure their wins or their careers like [Alberto] Contador or [Bradley] Wiggins. They have learnt that it's

below Winners, like Craig Alexander, leave no stones unturned.

above Roche believes that not everybody can become a winner.

structured. They don't go out to ride a race and win the race. They go out and analyse their itinerary, they plan the places where they can afford to lose time, where they hope to gain time. The don't just go, put a number on their back and ride. They go there committed and they have their strategy all determined before they get out there. The one thing these guys have in common is that they're natural winners.

But can anyone become a 'winner'? Roche isn't sure.

❝ **It's something** that you can get used to. I think if you are not a winner it's very difficult to become one. It's something that you have – you can develop it and get better. But when people have it in their mind and mentality then they don't settle for second place and they can just drive, drive, drive and they want to win. If

you haven't got it in your mentality you can try to win, do your best, and you will win races but I think it's a lot easier if you have that mentality.

That drive to win is what propelled Roche up the mountain in La Plagne (as we discussed in Chapter 10 – Adaptation). It's what gave him the legs to ride away from the group after 277.5km of the 278km UCI Road World Championships in Austria. And it's what drove him to contravene team orders and ride solo to the Maglia Rosa in the Giro d'Italia.

❝ **When you're getting it** really hard it's about digging in, thinking about the win and all the hard work you've put into it, and being very tough on yourself and not tapping yourself because you won or you came second.

To me it's win. It's not about numbers, it's about winning. End of story.

Champions *forget*

Roche and Alexander might differ in their approach to performance, but they share a very common trait: neither man rests on his laurels. In fact, they share an approach to winning that has been echoed by many famous champions, both in endurance sports and away from them. Alexander reflects:

❝ **I have a short memory.** I'm not really interested in looking back and admiring what's on the mantelpiece other than from the perspective of trying to learn from the performance. I'll admire all of that when my career is over. The motivation for me is the same as it's always been: to fulfil the simple commitment I made to be the best athlete I can be.

Roche is in a different stage of his career than Alexander. Having retired from cycling in 1993 he now enjoys the luxury of looking back on his titles and wins. During his career, though, he refused to do that.

SHIMANO
RUSSIAN CYCLING FEDERATION
A.NYCH
A524TO 197
RUSSIA
ITERA

❝ **When I won** the Giro I took a car and drove home to Paris. I was in Paris at six in the morning and then at half past eight I was buying croissants before going out training again and preparing for the Tour. I won the Tour and I was on a plane the next day for a reception and then back to Holland racing the next day preparing for the Worlds. So I was always going forwards irrespective of the results of one event. Winning the event, losing the event or whatever, I was always on to the next one.

Sometimes I admire people who can win events, have a party and let their hair down. Whereas my negative – or positive – side is that I didn't take a lot of time to celebrate my achievements. But at the same time it minimised what I was doing as well because I looked even stronger for the next event. I wasn't really happy with anything. That's a good thing in sport: to achieve the maximum you've got to be always going, going, going.

above Some of the best athletes in the world refuse to acknowledge wins until they retire.

opposite Professional cycling is one of the most gruelling sports on the planet.

This is the kind of attitude that helps to define the good from the great. They are constantly working to improve themselves and looking forward to the next race. Just as they are constantly hungry to win.

Winning is a mentality. Both Craig Alexander and Stephen Roche – men who have won the biggest races in their respective sports – recognise that. What's more, winning is about so much more than simply getting your head down and going for it. It is the pursuit of perfection in performance (even if that perfection is realised through an 'ugly' win). Whether the motivation emanates from the desire to execute the perfect race, or finds its base in the aggressive pursuit of victory, winners share a number of key traits. They are meticulous in their preparation. They are unflinching in their drive. They have an ability to push their bodies to their absolute limit, and occasionally they go beyond them. And they are driven to win. Not to compete, but to win. And when all of that comes together, as it has done for Alexander and Roche on numerous occasions, the pain of winning feels 'sweet'.

WINNING: KEY POINTS

- Winning in endurance sports does not necessarily entail crossing the line first. For many athletes, successfully completing a challenge is equal to winning.
- Winners prepare meticulously for races and determine their strengths and weaknesses relative to their opponents.
- Sport is not personal. Defeating an opponent does not mean that you do not respect them, just that you were better than them on the day.
- There is a big difference between wanting to do your best and wanting to win.
- Winners forget: many sporting champions refuse to acknowledge their achievements until the end of their careers.

14

When it all comes together

Throughout this book we have looked at different strategies and scenarios that athletes of all abilities can draw on in the pursuit of mental strength. In this final chapter we are going to look at a single example of how various theoretical principles on building mental strength and confidence can be applied to a specific race-day scenario.

At the London 2012 Olympics Nicola Spirig was forced to call on every ounce of her mental strength to walk away with the Gold medal in triathlon. It was the culmination of years of intense mental and physical work – and the perfect example of what happens when an athlete gets it right on the day (even when things aren't necessarily going her way).

Going for *Gold*
NICOLA SPIRIG

The sport of triathlon has never witnessed anything like it. Hundreds of thousands of spectators lined the streets of London to watch one the few public races of the 2012 Olympics. While the majority of banners were unfurled in support of the home favourite Helen Jenkins, the crowd cheered every one of the 55 athletes who took to the waters of the Serpentine in London's Hyde Park on 4 August. Few could have predicted that they were about to witness the closest finish in Olympic triathlon history. Even fewer knew what eventual Gold medallist Nicola Spirig had gone through on her road to Olympic glory.

THE PREPARATION

Nicola Spirig discovered her passion for triathlon as a child and quickly developed into a world-class athlete. But she wanted more. To achieve that, she realised that she had to be physically and mentally stretched. Recognising that her father, who was her coach and had done a great job of developing her as an athlete for 15 years, was not the right person to push her further, she made the decision to join the squad of controversial Australian coach Brett Sutton. It wasn't an easy choice for Spirig to make. She openly admits that she had doubts about Sutton both before – and during – the early stages of their coaching relationship, although she now

Nicola **SPIRIG**

" It didn't matter if I had nothing in my legs any more, I just knew that I had to find something somewhere to get to the finish line first. It didn't matter where I took it from or how I did it, it just mattered that I got to that finish line first.

recognises the huge influence that the Australian has had on her development as an athlete.

" I was working with my father as my coach for 15 years until after my first Olympics, and then after that from 2006 I was working with Brett Sutton. It was an amazing time and I learnt a lot. He taught me that I not only had to improve physically, but also that I had to change my mentality. You could say that I had to be a little bit less Swiss and a little bit more Australian – really giving 100 per cent and not being too modest. Trying to win the Gold medal and not just trying to win a medal and just being good. It took me a long time to actually realise that he was right and that I had to change.

It took a long time, and it took a lot of work on both sides. Sutton is characteristically forthright about the development of their relationship, describing it as something of a 'war'.

" The first year of training was one email after another between us, of me getting contradicted by her, and of me saying 'this is what we need to do'. At that stage she was doubting whether she should train with me.

Part of the conflict arose because Sutton recognised that for Spirig to realise her ambitions he would have to train more than just her body – he would have to overhaul her mental approach to the sport.

" The problem was she believed that she wasn't strong enough and she had tendencies to prophesise that. I had seen her do things that were so tough, but when she did them she didn't think that they were tough. So she would never give herself kudos, it was always: 'knock myself, knock myself, knock myself, I'm not good enough, I'm not good enough' and then when I told her certain things were weak, the hard part of it was that I would say 'but you're so strong in some areas' and she would say 'No, I'm not good enough.' So basically from a very early time we started to go to work on that psychologically, and that meant early on we were at war.

above Nicola Spirig was in dominant form going into the Olympics.

I had to work out what parts of her personality could work for her, and I found that the things that were working against her were the things that I could get working for her in the future. She was always judging

above 'Just get out there and give it a fling, you've done the training' – Brett Sutton.

herself harshly, was always a perfectionist – she still is. I had to change that around and say to myself that she could use those qualities to be a positive rather than a negative. She realises that now. Nicola Spirig in 2012 is not the same Nicola Spirig of 2006 – and I just don't mean athletically. As a person she's different as well; she had to change her racer's personality.

In Sutton's mind, Nicola Spirig the Olympic champion certainly took a while to develop. However, within six months of her joining Sutton's squad there had been a discernible improvement in results. Throughout 2005 and 2006, Spirig's form had been erratic, the Swiss athlete finishing outside the top ten in the majority of the ITU races that she competed in (she was outside the top ten in five of seven ITU races in 2005, and five of six ITU races in 2006). In 2007, though, things were on the up. Spirig finished inside the top ten in nine of the 12 ITU races that she competed in, and scored her first ITU World Cup victory. She was starting to realise her potential. 2008 – an Olympic year – saw another solid set of results (Spirig did not finish outside the top ten in any ITU race) and she finished sixth at the Beijing Olympics.

With 2008 done, it was time to focus on the London 2012 Olympics. Gold was the goal (although Spirig probably would not have admitted it at the time), and four years out Spirig and Sutton started to draw up a plan on how to realise that ambition.

❝ *I needed the* experience from the two former Olympics in 2004 and 2008 to actually win the Gold medal at the London Olympics. Just to realise what it needs, to know what to expect from the Olympics and how to handle the pressure and the special situation – the Olympics is always special. If you look at the previous winners at the Games, well there are more surprise winners at the Olympics than in other situations – like a world championships. For me it was a whole journey.

The first part of their four-year plan saw Spirig make the unconventional move of taking a step back from the sport for two years. She was still competing – Spirig secured two European championship titles in 2009 and 2010, plus a raft of ITU victories – but she also decided to focus on completing her law degree.

❝ *After Beijing in 2008* I decided to go back to university. Long-term it was clear that I would finish my law studies in 2010 so I would have two years to prepare for the 2012 Olympics. It was a long-term goal. It all was planned. Studying meant that I couldn't concentrate 100 per cent on sport for two years, but it was also really important to me to have finished my studies and have a good education. That was a little detail which helped me afterwards to do my sports and concentrate on the Olympics and know that whatever happened I had a good education and could go on regardless of whether I got last or first at the Olympics.

Spirig could argue that the decision to focus on her studies meant that she was not building to London 2012 until two years out from the race. However, it is possible to counter that by arguing that completing her studies was an essential element in her winning the Gold medal. It was a necessary step to alleviating the pressure that she was putting on herself.

The Olympic Games is a rare opportunity for athletes in many sports to shine. Going into London 2012 Spirig had competed at two Olympics, and she is currently considering going for a spot in the Swiss team at Rio 2016. If she realises that goal she will be one of the few triathletes to have competed at four Olympic Games

below Spirig believed she needed the experience of Beijing to win in London.

(at the London 2012 Games, Anja Dittmer was the only female triathlete to have competed at four Games, Simon Whitfield and Hunter Kemper are the only men to have done so). With at best just four attempts to medal at a Games (and by Spirig's reckoning it is hard to do so without prior Olympic experience) the pressure is immense. Add to that the buzz around the Games, the attention and the unfamiliarity of places like the athletes' village and you begin to understand why it is not uncommon to see athletes choking on the biggest stage of them all.

As such, Spirig's decision to back up her athletic career with a law degree helped to take some of that pressure off her. Of course, there was still expectation and nerves. But there was also a normality to her life – the Olympics was not the be-all and end-all. Whether or not she was aware of it at the time, this grounded perspective on the Games was a piece of the puzzle that would help her to relax and focus on race day. Relaxation was key, and something that Sutton hammered home on the eve of the race itself.

> ❝ *I kept saying to her:* 'Your mother is still going to love you on Sunday morning so who gives a shit? Just get out there and give it a fling, you've done the training.'

As mentioned, Spirig was still competing – and winning major events – while studying for her degree. The fact that she could split her focus between both is testament to her talent as an athlete. However, once the law degree was complete, she was 100 per cent focused on getting on to the podium at London 2012. At this point it is important to note that it was only when she was coming to the end of her training period that Spirig started to aim for Gold. At the beginning, the podium was enough.

> ❝ *I never had* a lot of self-confidence so I was never the one from the beginning who said 'I want to win the Gold medal at the Olympics.' I had to build up to that and I really needed Brett's help for that. I always had moments when I doubted and that's why I was so glad

to have Brett on my side because it is easy to believe in yourself and believe that you can reach your goals if you have a person who you trust and you know that he understands the business of the sport.

Throughout her training, both in the years that she was studying and the two years leading up to the Games, Sutton was constantly working on her attitude. As well as brutal training regimen that saw her swimming up to 60 kilometres a week, Sutton was trying to instil in her the mental strength to win.

> ❝ *She's very clinical.* So she'll quote to you what I said to her in 2008 and give you the date. I find that very hard because I'm a very non-specific guy so if I start saying something, even now, she'll say 'In 2008 on 24 May you told me this.' It's incredible, but that's the way the Swiss are. They'll beat you up, but they can't improvise and overcome when things don't go their way.
>
> If she was a boxer she would get knocked out in the second round of every fight she had. I used to use boxing terminology and say 'You have to improvise and overcome, you get hurt sometimes, you can't do what you want to do, you have to bide your time.' I use a lot of boxing terminology because it's very true. How fast you train doesn't mean anything once someone has smacked you in the face. You've got to have survival instincts and she didn't have any. If she wasn't hitting the numbers she would panic, and let the panic and desire to be good destroy her. What I was trying to point to with the Australian comment [when he told Spirig to be less Swiss and more Australian] is the 'she'll be all right' attitude. You know: 'I'm getting a good kicking but I'll hang in and see if I can turn it around.' Whereas her mentality was more 'It's not happening today, so it's not my day.' What I tried to point out to her was that she had been to two Olympics and lots of world championships and why hadn't she succeeded? Because she was waiting for the perfect storm. She was waiting for everything to click on the big day.

above Spirig's legs began to cramp towards the end of the bike leg.

I took that away and said 'I don't care if on the big day you have a shocker, it's up to us to train so that you can have a bad day and stand on the Olympic podium.' That was our mantra for the last three years. It was that we're not training to have a great day at the Olympics, but we're training to be so good that if we have a bad day we can still get on the podium. That was something she could hang on to because it was not a set number. She's a set-number person, so when she's not hitting them she over-tries and it starts to get worse and then she panics and then the wheels fall off.

The approach was perhaps not as laissez-faire as Sutton makes out. Spirig needed numbers to be able to realise her potential. In training she got them. In fact, Sutton produced numbers that the Swiss star simply did not believe that she could hit. Trawling back through the training plans of world champion triathletes that he had previously coached like Emma Carney and Emma

Snowsill (who won Gold in Beijing 2008), Sutton reproduced sets of numbers that he believed would propel Spirig to Olympic Gold.

❝ I would say to Nicola: 'This is her training, this is what she was doing to run that time, Nicola.' She would say: 'I can't do that time.' And I would go back: 'But you're doing the same speeds and faster than she was in training so why shouldn't you be able to do this time?' And she would say: 'Because of this and that.' In her own mind, she was giving me the negative feedback and it was sinking in.

So I would say to her: 'Emma Carney has run a 15:50, who in triathlon runs a 15:50?' 'Nobody.' 'Good, well here is what she used to do, here are her sessions, I want you to make these.' Of course, three years out she was nowhere near it and she said 'that's impossible' and I said 'we'll work towards it'. So of course it was impossible, then highly improbable, then improbable, then probable and then come January/February she started to hit some of the numbers and by June she was nailing everything. The confidence just grew and grew and grew and when we did our last track set she just nailed it better than anybody that I have ever trained and I looked at her and said 'We're ready – nobody can beat you. If you have a shocking day nobody can get you off the podium so let's just forget about it and have fun.' During the last month we never talked about it.

Tough training sessions combined with hard 'tune-up' races had helped instil in Nicola Spirig an unwavering confidence in her own ability. While a lot of other athletes went into a period of racing 'hibernation' ahead of the Olympics, Spirig did quite the opposite. She won three of the five ITU races that she entered – including one

European championship. She also won Ironman 70.3 Rapperswil (1.9km swim, 90km bike, 21.1km run – double the bike and run distance she would have to race in London) just two months out from the Olympics, the Swiss 5km track championships just four weeks before the Games and another 70.3 in Antwerp just 13 days ahead of her race in London. Sutton was confident that Spirig now possessed the mental and physical strength required to realise her goals.

" **She wrote a couple** of articles that said 'I think I'll fail if I haven't got on the podium.' She never used to put that type of stuff on herself – she was very against that type of thinking. But when she started to talk like that you start to realise that she's gaining her confidence. That was the key.

THE RACE

The build-up to the race in London wasn't plain sailing for Spirig. In the final days before the biggest race of

below The favourites all emerged from the water together at London 2012.

her career she started getting stitches and cramps in her legs, but didn't think too much about them. The preparation had gone well and both athlete and coach were confident that Spirig could perform on the day. Sutton reflects:

> ❝ **I was very confident** that she was going to win and when she got sick I was still confident. She did win having a shocker – she had a bad race. She had cramp problems and had had them for two or three days before the race. And that's why she changed her tactics – there was no way in the world she should have won that race. She did everything upside down and she did it because she was sick.

Nicola Spirig was able to win the race because of the physical and mental work that she had done in the lead up to it. The tough training regimen had instilled in her a belief that she could win the Olympics, and she could do it even against significant adversity (not to mention a stellar field).

> ❝ **I felt for good** for the race – I had minor issues but nothing too bad.
>
> I started the swim and the swim was hard. It's always hard for me as it's my weakest discipline and I never really know where I am. I was quite relieved when I got out of the water with all of the major athletes who would play a part in the race – [Helen] Jenkins, [Lisa] Nordén, [Emma] Moffatt and [Erin] Densham – they were all right beside me so I knew that I had had a decent swim and I could go from there and have all of the cards in my hand.

A lot of the talk ahead of the race had focused on the athletes from two countries: Great Britain and Australia. Great Britain received significant attention for employing a *domestique* in the form of Lucy Hall. Hall – a strong swimmer/biker – was supposed to help Jenkins break away from the rest of the field. However, despite the young Brit opening up a significant advantage in the water, Jenkins was unable to swim with her and so

emerged alongside the other pre-race favourites. The Australian team had suffered because of a selection debacle that was not resolved until just weeks before the Olympics. In the end, one of the athletes Sutton feared most – reigning Olympic champion and former Sutton squad member Emma Snowsill – was not selected for the team. The Australians still had Emma Moffatt and Erin Densham, who were both capable of winning, but Moffatt fell early on during the bike and retired, while Densham pushed Spirig all the way to the finish line, eventually taking Bronze.

❝ **I did quite a lot** of work on the bike because I was the only one who got the riders to attack back, and that took some energy. But I knew I was a good bike rider and it wouldn't hurt me that much. I started to have a few signs of cramp at the end of the bike. That was really unusual for me.

At this point, Brett Sutton – who was sitting in a bookmakers close to Hyde Park betting on his 'horse' – is very clear about what he thinks would have happened had they not done so much work together.

❝ **Nicola Spirig** four years ago wouldn't have finished the race. Nicola Spirig two years ago would have run top ten. Nicola Spirig 18 months ago would have held on for fifth or 12 months ago got third, but it all just kept evolving. Every year she got better, she got harder and mentally stronger.

Instead of letting the cramps derail her bid for Olympic Gold, Spirig recognised that she needed to adapt her strategy and work out what she had to do to realise her minimum expectation: a podium finish.

❝ **I got off the bike** and tried to just run with the first pack – with whoever was leading – and I tried to drink a bit to get control of the cramps. They kind of stayed so I never felt completely comfortable running but I was relieved that the pace wasn't too high – I could stay with the first pack without too many problems. We got closer and closer to the finish line and I knew

that the sprint was one of my strengths and I knew that some of the other athletes had attacked before and I knew that if I was still there with one kilometre to go they didn't have much of a chance. So the longer I could stay with the first pack, the bigger my chances got to win the Gold medal. So we just ran and athletes started to drop away – in the end there was just four of us.

And I was still scared about the cramps because every time I had to turn around or go up the hill or do a slight change of direction or react to something my muscles reacted and cramped up again. The one thing I was scared about was if someone attacked at the finish and I had to react really quickly then the cramps would get really bad. That's why I basically decided not to wait until the last 200 metres like I planned to do but to attack quite early and build up and build up and hope the others would fall off. It was not planned like that – I knew that it wasn't my biggest strength – but it was the best option that I had with the problems that I had. So that's why I was the one changing the pace and attacking really early. And I think that's why it got so close at the end.

It couldn't have been any closer. Spirig and Nordén were shoulder to shoulder down the finishing chute, and the Olympic timing chips couldn't separate the pair on the line.

❝ **The sprint was** too long for me but I was so determined to win that I didn't let her overtake at the end. There was a screen in front of me so I saw that Lisa [Nordén] was getting closer again. Again Brett was really helpful with preparing mentally. It didn't matter if I had nothing in my legs any more, I just knew that I had to find something somewhere to get to the finish line first. It didn't matter where I took it from or how I did it, it just mattered that I got to that finish line first.

Anyone who watched that race will remember the end of it. They will remember the minutes that followed as commentators, athletes and officials tried to work out who had managed to cross the line first. Even the photograph wasn't conclusive (the Swedish Olympic Federation referred the decision to award the Gold to Spirig to the Court of Arbitration for Sport, who upheld the decision). In those minutes, as Spirig and Nordén waited for the result, the 'Sutton-effect' was again in evidence.

> ❝ *It was the big question:* who won? Those minutes when we didn't know were really hard. After the finish I looked at Lisa and she looked at me and we both thought that I would be first. So I was feeling that I was first but of course I wanted an official to confirm that. I asked about four or five people and nobody could answer me. And in the end Lisa said 'I'm happy about the medal, it doesn't matter which one' and I kind of agreed but it's different if you're celebrating a Gold or celebrating a Silver medal so it was hard to be happy until I knew which one it was.

The rest is history. Nicola Spirig was crowned Olympic champion, claiming one of the two Gold medals that Switzerland would win at the Games. It had been a blistering finale to an enthralling race. But with her back against the wall and the strategy out the window, how did Spirig dig so deep and push on through to take the Gold medal?

> ❝ **We physically trained** the finish a lot of times in a lot of sessions and I trained with guys who were better than me so I really knew how to sprint. I had sprinted against Lisa before – in Kitzbuhel about a month and a half before the Olympics. So I was prepared for that and I was mentally prepared as well. Brett and I had discussed it many times. I knew each of the three athletes running with me, what their strengths were, if they were fast in a 600-metre sprint, 400-metre sprint or 200-metre sprint, I knew exactly how they would react and I prepared everything.
>
> What helped me a lot was that we had discussed the mental side and I knew that when there was just four athletes, I couldn't think about just winning a medal and not getting fourth because that would have

above Helen Jenkins of Great Britain tried to push ahead in the swim leg.

meant that I was fighting for third or second and not about winning first and taking risks fighting for the Gold. So I really had to focus on Gold and I really had to think that it was the only medal I wanted and I would risk everything to win the Gold medal and not just run for not getting fourth. I think that was really important for the win.

The other thing was that I had sprinted against Lisa before, and we both knew that normally I was the better sprinter and I think that gave me a lot of confidence and probably made her doubt herself a little bit and react too late – just a second or two. I think at first she didn't believe that she could beat me, or she was doubting it, and in the end when she saw that I was not getting faster any more towards the finish she was too late.

Sutton has a different opinion on the final sprint and whether or not Lisa Nordén would have beaten Spirig on the day.

> ❝ *I think at the finish* – to be honest, everyone thinks differently from me – the other girl not only ran out of room but also out of the sprint. I think they could have run for another 150 metres and Nicola

would have pulled away. She was spent but the other girl was too. The other girl didn't do a thing all race which was perfect training and perfect competition tactics. She didn't have a go on the bike, she waited on the run. She did Nicola's tactics: we were going to wait until the last 300 metres and then go bang. Because of the circumstances Nicola changed the tactics on the race day and she still got home. I just think she would have kept finding something because she is a terrific athlete.

While those conversations are relatively redundant in light of the result, they are a reflection on the strategy, strength and will to overcome that are an essential weapon in every endurance athlete's race-day armoury. For years Spirig had waited for a 'perfect storm' of race-day conditions that would allow her to realise her ambitions. Had she not put in the months and years of

hard work she would not have had the mental strength to overcome an imperfect storm of conditions that could have quite easily left her ruing a missed opportunity. Instead, Nicola Spirig is the Olympic champion and she always will be.

Spirig's was a journey that changed both her life and that of her coach:

❝ **Nicola may have** become a better athlete for knowing me but I know for sure I walked away a better coach for knowing her. The force of her personality and her determination not to let me dominate her allowed us both to become better. The Swiss Miss is a champion with a fully balanced life, with time for sport, study and family. It was an incredible journey for both of us.

CONCLUSION

Nicola Spirig's metamorphosis from being a regular top-ten finisher to being the best in the world illustrates the fundamental importance of mental strength in endurance sports. If we start with the premise that the gruelling training regimen that Spirig was subjected to gave her the physical tools to perform on the day, we can see how the different elements of a strong mental attitude come into play.

With a clearly defined goal established years in advance, she had a carefully constructed training plan that would allow her to peak for the right race at the right time. The training gave her the confidence, but it also made her believe in herself and her abilities. This belief was translated into improved performance, which further instilled the belief in herself as an athlete. Spirig had a clearly defined strategy going into the race itself, but was forced to adapt that strategy because of the adverse situation that she was faced with (cramps). In essence, she was focusing on the aspects of her performance that she could directly control, and she was good enough to ensure that that would be enough to secure her minimum objective (a podium finish). Finally, she was propelled to the Gold medal by her unwavering mental strength and will to win. While the former can be taught, it is much more difficult with the latter. In fact, that will to win is very often the difference between the very good and the very best.

As a case study, Nicola Spirig's Gold at the London 2012 Olympics highlights what can be achieved with hard work and dedication. And while only a very select few will ever have the opportunity to claim Gold at an Olympics or win a world championship, we can all work hard towards our personal goals and victories. With the right level of dedication and commitment, it is possible to realise your ambitions – however hard it might seem when you start out on the journey.

below The race was tight from start to finish.

CONCLUSION

IT ALL COMES DOWN TO CONFIDENCE

Many athletes set out on the endurance sports journey completely focused on developing the physical aspect of their performance. That is understandable; when athletes make the decision to commit to a race they do so because they want to challenge themselves in terms of distance or time. Because of this, they focus on developing their physical strength, often paying little heed to their mental preparation.

This is a mistake.

Endurance events will challenge more than just your body; they will test your mind too. As a result, if you want to be ready to realise your race-day goals you have to be mentally prepared. You have to be confident.

Confidence is something that every athlete – pretty much every human being – strives towards. At its most basic it can be defined as:

1. The state of feeling certain about the truth of something.
2. A feeling of self-assurance arising from one's appreciation of one's own abilities or qualities.

While these two definitions (there are plenty more in the dictionary) capture what many athletes aim for, actually having that confidence to realise your goals is a very different thing indeed. It takes time and it takes work to truly believe that you are capable of achieving your objectives.

Being confident in yourself is not easy. It is certainly not as simple as just telling yourself – or the world, for that matter – how good you are at doing something. Nor is it about just staying positive or forging your own path and ignoring the feedback of others. Rather, it is about working hard and adopting the right attitude to become the 'complete' athlete – regardless of the level at which you are competing. It is about doing what it takes to truly believe that you are capable of realising your goals.

Of course, a huge part of that confidence comes from the training that you will inevitably be putting in during your endurance sports career. For months – and in some cases years – you will be building towards a single event (or maybe a series of events). The fatigue will, at times, be intense. And the sheer demands placed on you by your training schedule may occasionally feel quite overwhelming. But know this: all of the hours and all of the miles that you

are devoting towards this singular aim will provide you with the foundations for the confidence that will ultimately drive you towards the finish line.

But just as you spend time developing the physical side of your performance, you must also work on the mental aspect of it. Because regardless of whether you are a novice, a nationally ranked amateur athlete or even a professional, many of the miles that you put into training will be wasted if they are not backed up by the right mental attitude and the confidence that you can deliever on your objectives.

Throughout this book we have looked at various techniques and strategies that will help to build your race-day confidence. Establishing an effective set of goals will give you targets to aim for throughout the training phase, and will develop your confidence as your ability improves. Finding a balance in this training phase will help you to maintain a positive attitude, which will have a direct impact on your athletic performance. Adopting mental techniques to prepare your mind for racing will enable you to realise your physical potential. As will the knowledge that you can

adapt your strategy or employ techniques to help you push through difficult periods in training or racing. Independently, adopting these various approaches to endurance sports will help to build your confidence in your own ability. But as the athletes interviewed throughout the book have demonstrated, when used together, they will provide you with a formidable armoury with which to realise your athletic potential.

Confidence is not an easy thing to establish. What's more, it is not simply a case of 'once you have it, it's there for ever'. Like so many of the concepts that we have looked at in this book, it is constantly evolving. As an athlete, you will be forced to evolve with it.

The best athletes in the world train and prepare their bodies and minds so that they can realise their goals. Although your goals might be different, your approach doesn't have to be. If you attack endurance sports with the right attitude, then you will stand on the start line with the knowledge that you are in the best physical and mental shape to realise the targets that you have set yourself. That is how you will win. That is how you will have the mental strength to be the best that you can be.

References

Brailsford, Dave. Television interview. BBC. London.
8 August 2012.

Jones, Graham (2002): 'What is this thing called mental toughness? An investigation of elite sport performers', *Journal of Applied Sport Psychology*, 14:3, 205–218

Middleton, S.C., Marsh, H.M., Martin, A.J., Richards, G.E. and Perry, C. (2005): 'Discovering mental toughness: a qualitative study of mental toughness in elite athletes', *Psychology Today*, 22, 60–72

Picture credits

Photography pages: 5 (top) and 127 © Bruno Ismael Silva Alves/Shutterstock; 5 (bottom), 36, 79 and 154 © Jeff Lim C.W./Shutterstock; 5 (second from top), 42, 54, 81 and 131 © Rihardzz/Shutterstock; 5 (third from top), 88, 134 (right) and 135 © Tami Freed/Shutterstock; 5 (fourth from top) and 104 © AFP/Getty Images; 8 (right) and 77 © Craig Alexander; 8 (left) and 37 © Elaine Thompson/AP/PA Images; 9 (left and second from left), 48, 50, 51, 52 (left and right) © RAF/Crown Copyright; 9 (third from left) © Dee Caffari; 9 (right), 110 and 111 © Chris Ison/PA Archive/PA Images; 10 (left), 15 (first in mosaic) © Sandra Mu/Getty Images; 10 (second from left), 27, 45 and 46 © Chris Stewart/AP/ Press Association Images; 10 (third from left) and 133 © Lizzie Edmonds/PA Archive/PA Images; 10 (right), 137 and 139 © Eddie Clark; 11 (left) © Hincapie Sportswear; 11 (middle), 82 and 89 © Chad Riley; 11 (right), 32, 49, 87 and 103 © David McNew/Getty Images; 12 (left) and 113 © Rendy Opdycke; 12 (middle) and 145 © Peter Muhly/AFP/Getty Images; 12 (right), 123 and 152 © Nutan/Gamma-Rapho/Getty Images; 13 (left and second from the left) and 125 © Craig Kolesky; 13 (third from the left) and 14 (left) © Nicola Spirig; 13 (right), 158 and 159 © Maxisport/Shutterstock. com; 14 (right), 15 (third in mosaic), 34, 93, 96–97, 99 and 102 © Samo Vidic/Getty Images; 14 (middle), © Brittany Trubridge; 15 (left and bottom left) and 141 © Doug Pensinger/Getty Images Sport; 15 (second in mosaic) © Beelde Photography/Shutterstock; 15 (fourth in mosaic) and 67 © Fabrice Coffrini/AFP/Getty Images; 15 (fifth in mosaic) and 169 © AFP/Getty Images; 16–17 © Tamara Kulikova/Shutterstock; 18–19 © Brent Winebrenner/Lonely Planet Images/Getty Images; 20–21 © Maxim Petrichuk/Shutterstock; 22 © Marc Pagani Photography/Shutterstock; 23 (bottom left) © Neale Cousland/Shutterstock; 23 (bottom right)

© Geoff Nelson/Shutterstock; 23 (top) © Kaliva/ Shutterstock; 24, 41, 69, 72, 73, 83 and 134 (left) © Radu Razvan/Shutterstock; 28 © Jacques Boissinot/ The Canadian Press/PA Images; 29 © Mike Wintroath/ AP/Press Association Images; 31 © Peter M. Fredin/AP/ PA Images; 33 and 160 © Martin Good/Shutterstock; 37 © Yoann MORIN/Shutterstock; 53, 124 and 126 © Richard Thornton/Shutterstock; 56, 129 and 170–171 © Shutterstock; 57, 100, 164–165 and 168 © Stefan Holm/Shutterstock; 58 © Chris Stewart/AP/PA Images; 59 © Thomas Frey/DPA/PA Images; 61 and 149 © Alvis Upitis/Getty Images; 62 and 156 © Malgorzata Kistryn/ Shutterstock; 63 © Bruce Raynor/Shutterstock; 64–65 © AFP/Getty Images; 66 and 147 © Hyoung Chang/ Denver Post/Getty Images; 70 © Rodger Bosch/AFP/ Getty Images; 74–75 and 148 © Chris Stewart/AP/PA Images; 77 © hinnamsaisuy/Shutterstock; 79 and 101 © Lawrence Wee/Shutterstock; 80 and 146 © Alberto Loyo/Shutterstock; 84–85 and 115 © Stephen Pond/Getty Images; 91 © BKingFoto / Shutterstock; 92 © lukeurbine/Shutterstock; 94 © FCG/Shutterstock; 105 © Martynova Anna/Shutterstock; 106 and 114 © Carsten Medom Madsen/Shutterstock; 107 © Sergey Orlov/Shutterstock; 108 © Marcel Mochet/AFP/Getty Images; 116 © Lilyana Vynogradova/Shutterstock; 117 © Nigel Roddis/Getty Images; 119 © Tina Fineberg/ AP/PA Images; 120 © Lorimer Images/Shutterstock; 121 © Stephen Roche; 132 © Mahe Bertrand/ABACA/PA Images; 138 © Mike Hall; 142 © Chris Carlson/AP/PA Images; 143 © Francesco Carucci/Shutterstock; 144 © patrimonio designs ltd/Shutterstock; 151 © Stringer/AFP/Getty Images; 155 © conde/ Shutterstock; 157 © luca85/Shutterstock; 161 © PA Wire/PA Archive/PA Images; 163 © Andrew Milligan/ PA Archive/PA Images; and 167 © Daniel Goodings/ Shutterstock.

Index